PRODUCTIVITY SECRETS FOR ENTREPRENEURS WHO WORK AT HOME

PRODUCTIVITY SECRETS FOR ENTREPRENEURS WHO WORK AT HOME

Leslie Ann Cardinal, M.Ed.

The Cardinal Success Book Series

Disclaimer & Copyright Information

The examples in the book are offered in an effort to bring the concepts to life and to offer encouragement to the reader. The names and minor details have been changed to protect the privacy of the people involved.

The opinions expressed in this book are not a guarantee of results because your results are determined by your own efforts and decisions. The ideas and opinions in this book are not meant to take the place of legal, tax, medical, or other professional advice. If you need advice, please seek the help of a qualified professional.

ISBN-13: 978-172-3457449
ISBN-10 1723457442

Dedication

I'm delighted to dedicate this book to Janet Bonnin and Angela Woodrow, two longtime friends and colleagues who are both entrepreneurs who work at home. I admire you both so much for your determination and tenacity to keep your businesses moving forward and to persist in finding ways to be productive even in the face of challenges that home-based entrepreneurs encounter. You both have a wealth of experience and wonderful, caring hearts that you bring to your work. I know your customers and clients are blessed every day when they have the opportunity to work with you!

CONTENTS

Foreword..1

Introduction..5

SECTION ONE...**9**
WHAT IS PRODUCTIVITY WHEN YOU ARE WORKING AT HOME?

Chapter One...11
Many People Are Working At Home—Are You One of Them?

Chapter Two...17
What It Can Look Like For You To Work At Home

SECTION TWO...**23**
WHY PRODUCTIVITY IS A WORTHWHILE GOAL

Chapter Three..25
Reasons People Choose To Work at Home

Chapter Four...33
What Do You Hope to Accomplish By Working at Home?

SECTION THREE...**39**
WHAT IF YOU COULD DESIGN YOUR WORK AT HOME EXPERIENCE TO
MAXIMIZE YOUR PRODUCTIVITY?

Chapter Five..41
Creating Your Work Space At Home

Chapter Six...47
Tools and Equipment to Boost Your Productivity

Chapter Seven..53
Staying Energized and Healthy to Boost Your Productivity

Chapter Eight...61
Create Your Team

SECTION FOUR...**69**
HOW TO BE HIGHLY PRODUCTIVE WORKING AT HOME

Chapter Nine *71*
   Daily Action and Productivity Strategies

Chapter Ten *79*
   Tackling Big or Extended Term Projects

Chapter Eleven *85*
   Family Factors Matter, Especially When You Work at Home

Chapter Twelve...*91*
   Successful Ways to Handle Common Challenges

SECTION FIVE **101**
   WHAT'S NEXT ON YOUR WORK AT HOME JOURNEY?

Chapter Thirteen *103*
   The Next Stage: When Things Change or Evolve

Conclusion *109*

About the Author *111*

Foreword

Are you one of the growing number of entrepreneurs who work from home? Or perhaps you are in the 20 to 25% of employed adults who work from home? Or maybe you are one of the 80 to 90% who would like to work from home and wonder how and if you could manage it. Whichever group you fit into, this book, Leslie Cardinal's third and newest, is one you will want to read.

In *Productivity Secrets for Entrepreneurs Who Work at Home,* Leslie covers everything from considerations when deciding to work at home, to keeping yourself motivated, to accommodating your health needs, to systems for increasing your productivity. It's the A to Z of why and how to do it right!

I first met Leslie several years ago at a conference, and it didn't take long before we were exchanging not just contact information, but ideas on coaching, on business, and on life. It was obvious to me right away that she was sharing from a wealth of knowledge and experience. Even more important, she had a unique perspective on problem solving not just in the business side of entrepreneurship, but also in making the personal side work as well.

We have been friends and colleagues now for more than five years. Over those years, I have found that Leslie's suggestions and coaching are often different from other coaches I know. She has a richer perspective and background to draw on than most. In addition, being a perpetual student, she is always curious and interested in exploring new ideas and modalities with the intention of helping people achieve success and make life and work more satisfying and productive. As a lifelong learner myself, I recognize the effort it takes to keep up-to-date and to stay aware of current ideas that may help our clients and ourselves.

Now, of course, I know that the solutions Leslie suggests and the insightful questions she asks are often informed by her early studies in engineering and operations research. At that point in her career, she worked to optimize the connection between people and their work environment to maximize productivity. That experience, coupled with her degree in adult education, plus 17 years working from home as an entrepreneur—coach, trainer, consultant, author, and speaker— is the perfect combination of education and experience to write this book.

Over the years I've known Leslie, I've found her to have immense wisdom and experience about what is likely to work and what isn't. I've been impressed with her compassion, her clear vision, and her gumption in getting through her own challenges as a work-at-home businesswoman. When I met her, I was a fairly new work-at-home life coach and entrepreneur. All along the way, she has been unfailingly helpful and supportive. I've watched her navigate successfully through many issues that any home-based business person might have—procrastination, health issues, flagging motivation, family changes, unexpected death of a close colleague, and sadly, illness and death of a parent. Still she has kept her business afloat and thriving and she has managed to pivot and change direction when necessary.

People choose to work at home for many reasons. There are so many rewards in terms of convenience, freedom to live your life the way you want, flexibility to manage your time and energy as you choose, opportunity to make your own decisions, even being able to work in the environment that supports your energy and enhances your creativity and productivity. However, when you work at home, everything, including organizing the environment, scheduling, technology, finances, motivation, and productivity, is up to you. Leslie's brilliant book will be your best friend through it all.

Dorine Kramer, MD, MPH
www.YourTimeToSoar.com
Author of *Your Amazing Itty Bitty® Empty-Nesters Survival Handbook: 15 Critical Tips to Thrive When Your Kids Leave Home*

Introduction

You really can design your at-home business to fit your life and your style. This is a strong statement and it is the reason I am writing this book. I have been working at home for the past seventeen years. When I first left the corporate world, I was very excited to be able to work at home. I was delighted to be able to work in my own home and to grow my business at my own pace. I relished being able to look out the windows or to go outside for a few minutes to get some sunshine or to water the plants in my garden. After working in a busy and often noisy building with thousands of employees, I was excited to have the opportunity to plan and create my own work environment.

In my last corporate job, I traveled about 25% of the time with intense week-long trips to a variety of cities around the US. I enjoyed the opportunity to see other cities and I enjoyed the people I traveled to work with, but the glamour and excitement of travel began to wane after a while. I was also fortunate to work a four-day work week most of the time, but the days were long and started early. Because I am more of a night owl, it was a challenge to get enough sleep most nights.

When I first started working at home, it was a great relief to be able to adjust my schedule to better suit my needs. I was able to follow a better sleep schedule which boosted my energy. I was able to travel less, choosing to go to a few conferences and workshops each year.

I set up a couple of different areas in my house as places where I could work, just to have some variety. I experimented with different ways to schedule my time and my work. I also tried different methods to work in personal and household tasks without getting completely sidetracked by them.

Despite the benefits and pleasures of running a business from home, I also found there were challenges to making it work as well as I wanted it to. I was surprised at how many distractions there could be each day. This included everything from the ringing telephone to the temptation to run errands to the dishes in the sink that sometimes looked easier to tackle than the tough business project I needed to work on at the time.

And of course, since I was my own boss, I needed to be the one to set and maintain the priorities and to decide which of those top priorities to work on first and which to leave for later. As a solopreneur it was tempting to try to do all of the tasks myself even though I didn't enjoy some of them or do all of them equally well. And there were times when it was all too easy to procrastinate working on the priority tasks in favor of something easier or more fun.

Over the years, it has been amazing to see the ways that technology has advanced. The advent of social media, smartphones, and all kinds of apps has been exciting to watch. I've enjoyed but also felt challenged to quickly learn how to use them and to integrate them into my business in ways that make sense.

After a few years of working at home, I began to feel restless being isolated at home all day. This surprised me because I remembered how much I longed to be able to work at home during many of my years in the corporate world. I began to experiment with options for getting out of the house for a part of each day while still being able to get my work done. It was easy to fall into the trap of just escaping with the thought of running errands that were "needed" for the household. What I wanted was just a way to be able to be around more people and yet keep my business projects on track. I've developed ways to make a lot of my work portable, so I can get out of the house several times each week and still be productive in my business.

Over time my family's situation began to change too. My elderly parents began to have health challenges and to need more support and assistance. I encountered some of my own health challenges too, with recurring migraines. I needed to find ways to manage these personal and family needs while still being able to work and be productive.

As I talk with other entrepreneurs who work at home I hear a similar story. They enjoy the opportunity to work at home, but they find it very challenging too. Many of them face personal health issues or a family member who needs help and support some of the time. These entrepreneurs are eager to be successful, but they don't always know how to overcome some of the obstacles they encounter like distractions and procrastination.

These are the reasons I decided to write this book. I have experimented and found successful strategies to be productive while working at home. And in my coaching business, I have coached a wide variety of entrepreneurs through the process too. I'm excited to share the ideas and techniques that have worked for me and for my clients. It is my sincere hope you will find many strategies in this book that will help and encourage you on your entrepreneurial journey!

SECTION ONE

WHAT IS PRODUCTIVITY WHEN YOU ARE WORKING AT HOME?

When your goal is to be productive when you work at home, a good place to start is to clarify what it means to you. If you are reading this book, a couple of things may be true. You may already be working at home and looking to make your experience even better. Or you may be thinking about the idea of working at home and you want to explore how it could work for you and your business.

The first section of this book focuses on some of the background and history of the growing trend of people working at home. It covers some of the ways people work at home and how these kinds of arrangements are growing and evolving, especially as technology resources continue to expand.

Section One also covers what it could look like for you to work at home. It starts by looking at your current situation, whether you are already working at home or thinking about the option. It includes the possibility that working at home could help you to be even more productive than working in a traditional job setting.

As I talk with people who, like me, work from home, I find they almost all encounter similar challenges and benefits with this work arrangement. Most people would like to be more productive and they acknowledge that it is not as easy as they had hoped it would be. They usually want to continue to work at home, or need to, because of their circumstances.

They are looking for ways to be effective with getting more of their high value work tasks completed, while successfully blending in their personal and family needs too. They want to experience a sense of satisfaction and accomplishment and to minimize any sense of struggle with the process or disappointment with their results.

Whether you already work at home, or you are exploring the possibility, you'll begin to discover examples and stories of people in situations that may be similar to yours. Look for things you can relate to, such as challenges and opportunities that you see in your own setting. Look for ideas that will help you to find the encouragement and inspiration to make the work at home process rewarding and fulfilling for you.

Chapter One

Many People Are Working At Home—Are You One of Them?

Are you an entrepreneur working at home? Would you like to be able to join the growing number of people who are?

Many people are working at home now and finding that it is an excellent choice. They enjoy a wide range of benefits, from pursuing their key business goals, to setting their own best schedules, to taking care of important family and personal needs.

To make the most of working at home, it's important to find ways to be productive in the process. Even though there are many positive aspects of working at home, there are a variety of challenges too. This book can be a guide to you, helping you navigate these challenges and enjoy the benefits, while staying focused and productive.

History

In the past couple of decades there has been a growing number of people who work at home, or who want to work at home.

Often, this has meant pursuing some type of self-employment that could be based at home. It includes both full time as well as many part time options. Part time choices have been attractive because it allows time for other needs and priorities to fit into the schedule too. This can include family needs, health needs, and even other full or part-time work outside the home.

By the late 1980s, it was becoming more common to have a computer at home. Compared to what we have today, these were mostly simple computers that could do word processing, spreadsheets, and other basic functions. For a business at home, these computers made it possible to create professional looking letters, invoices and other documents. Being able to save a document on the computer made it possible to create a new version by simply modifying a past document, rather than having to type a completely new document on a typewriter.

In the mid-1990s, internet service became more widely available at home. This opened even more opportunities for working at home and being able to use technology in many ways, for research, content creation, connecting with people, and so much more.

Telephone technology began to advance in a variety of ways too. Originally, telephones were a fast way to connect, voice to voice, with customers, clients, and prospects. Businesses at home just had a landline telephone. Simple cell phones became more widely available, but they could only make phone calls or record voicemail messages. Smartphone technology was still in the future.

In 1996, I discovered the emerging profession of coaching. I wanted to pursue professional coach training to build on the training and leadership development skills that I already had. Even though I was employed full time I could see there might be opportunities to offer coaching services as a side business.

Coach University was one of two main schools that offered this type of coach training at that time. All of their courses were taught by teleseminar, and registration had to be completed online. This was very convenient because it meant I could take the classes from my home without having to travel for the training. But it also meant I would need to have internet access outside of work. This was the catalyst for me to sign up for internet access at home. Internet service was still very basic at that time, with dial up service as the main option. Having a computer and a simple cell phone and internet service at home opened the way for me to have more work at home options.

Current Trends

The current trend of people working at home is continuing to grow. There are likely a number of reasons for this. It can be less expensive for an employer to have some of their employees work from home. For example, there is less cost for office space, less cost for utilities, less need for parking spaces when employees work at home. Even if an employee comes to the office once or twice a week, many of these savings still occur.

It is often less expensive for the employee too. They don't have the cost of their commute to the office, they may be able to wear less expensive clothing some of the time, and they may be able to eat more of their meals at home. I saw examples of these types of arrangements among my coaching clients.

One of my clients, Sandy, took a new job that included working from home most of the time. The employer was located in another state and my client did not want to relocate and disrupt her family which was already established where she lived. Her new employer was willing for her to work from her home with the understanding that she would travel to the main office at regular intervals for face-to-face meetings.

Another client, Rita, owned her own business and had a traditional office with several employees. She looked at the trend for having employees work from home some of the time and felt that her business could make that work. When her office lease expired, she found a much smaller office space that was closer to her home. She furnished it with several work stations that her employees could use on the days when they worked in the office, but none of the employees had a permanent work station in the new office location. The employees had the flexibility to choose to work at home a little or a lot, as long as they were able to be effective in completing their work in an acceptable and timely way. This choice reduced Rita's expenses, offered more options to her employees, and ultimately helped to make the business attractive to a buyer.

For people who are self-employed, some of these same kinds of benefits and savings can occur. Your cost of housing is already being paid. You probably already have a computer and a printer and a cell phone that could be used for business purposes part of the time. And chances are, you already pay to have internet access at home that could be used for business too. In addition, having a business of your own may provide potential tax benefits too. (Discuss this with your accountant or tax adviser to see what may apply in your particular situation.)

There may be some additional considerations such as updating your homeowners insurance to cover your business activities, but this is very commonly available now. In addition there are some adjustments you may need to make to fit your business equipment and materials into your living space, and some changes to the way you use your time at home. I have a lot of creative ideas about ways you can meet these needs. We will go into these steps in more detail in the later chapters of this book.

Things Are Evolving

Computer and telephone technology is continuing to advance in remarkable ways. Smartphones also have more available apps and functionality than ever before. Computers are continuing to be more versatile and affordable every year. This makes many work-related tasks much more possible to do at home.

For example, I now use two laptops at home for my business. This happened out of necessity a couple of years ago. I had one laptop at the time and had it covered by a warranty. It developed a problem with the screen, and under the warranty I had to send it off to be repaired. I was told it would take about three weeks to complete the repair. When you run a business that relies on using your computer every day, being without it for three weeks is a real problem! I knew I had to find a solution quickly to keep my business running.

I immediately went out and bought another laptop, choosing a low cost but functional model. In fact, I purchased two identical laptop computers. It happened to be "Back to School" season and office supply stores were offering good prices. By buying two identical computers, I streamlined the learning curve that happens whenever you purchase new equipment. I had both laptops configured and running quickly, thanks to my tech person. (I highly recommend you find a tech person who can help you with these types of technical tasks if you are not naturally a techy person!)

Both computers are still running well. I use cloud storage such as Dropbox and Carbonite (for double backups, which is always a good idea). The other great benefit of cloud storage is that my files are available to me no matter which laptop I happen to be using. I can also access them from my smartphone or my iPad, if I need to.

If one of the laptops should have a major problem, my plan is to just buy another one, and keep on going. In fact, I learned that a number of business people do this. They buy a newer laptop every couple of years rather than waiting for a problem to occur. They use the new one to replace the oldest one. This way they always have fairly current computer technology for their business. It is also handy at times to be able to have two screens side by side for some of your projects such as for webinars.

I also chose to upgrade my iPhone to a newer version recently. My older iPhone was getting slower, wasn't keeping a charge as long, and didn't have the capacity for the apps, photos, videos, and podcasts that were becoming an increasing part of my business activities. To keep costs down, I chose a phone that isn't the very top of the line, but it still has much more functionality than the older and smaller phone than I had before.

Another simple upgrade I did a few years ago was to make the switch to a wireless printer. This makes it easy to work from a variety of places in the house and still print easily whenever needed. You can find inkjet printers and laser printers that do wireless printing. This also makes it easy to print from my iPhone or iPad as well.

You may find it helpful to follow some of these same trends in your at-home work arrangements. Keep an eye on the ways that phones and computers and other types of equipment are evolving. Most likely, you won't need to have the very latest or the most expensive equipment for your business to be successful. At the same time, don't hamper yourself unnecessarily with older equipment if newer equipment would really make a difference in your ability to be productive.

Wherever you are in your work at home journey, aim to be as satisfied and fulfilled and successful as you can. The goal is not just to be productive for the sake of being productive. The goal is bigger than that, to live your life in alignment with your values, and in ways that feel successful and fulfilling to you. Being productive is often a part of this as you use your skills and your resources to do things that make a difference and to enjoy a sense of accomplishment in the process.

Chapter Two

What It Can Look Like For You To Work At Home

Start with Your Goals

To be truly productive with your business you need to have clear goals. Your goals will guide you to make wise daily action choices that will be truly productive. You may already have a clear set of goals and a plan for your business. If so, congratulations! But if not, you are in good company. This is a good time to review your goals, or to create some if you need to.

When I coach with new clients, I always encourage them to start with identifying a handful of short term and longer term goals. For short term goals, I like to suggest that you choose three 90-day goals. Looking a bit further out, I recommend choosing three 3-year goals.

The reason I suggest 3-year goals as your longer term goals is that they are close enough in time to imagine completing them, and far enough out in time that you can accomplish some pretty exciting things. Technology is changing and evolving rapidly, and most small businesses also evolve within a 3 year period. Goals that are five or ten years out are harder to imagine or predict.

I also suggest that you have some 90-day goals because these shorter-term goals feel very real. In just 90 days you can make a lot of tangible progress toward these goals. If possible, break your 3-year goals into a series of 90-day goals so that you can see the connection between your current actions and your longer-term goals.

Write your goals down in your notebook. This makes it easy for you to review them regularly and to see your progress. It's also a great place for you to jot notes and ideas about how to pursue your goals. I also like to suggest that you write them on an index card or on a big sticky note and put it in a very visible place, someplace where you will see them often.

What's Your Current Situation?

Are you working at home now? Are you thinking about the possibility? Wishing you had the option to work at home or are you hesitant to consider it? Or have you been working at home but wish you had the option to work away from home more often? Take a moment to think about where you are now, with respect to the question of working at home. We'll talk about each of these situations in this chapter.

You may already be working at home, perhaps for many years, and yet you may have a feeling that you could be more productive in the process. It may be that your situation is changing and the methods that have been working for you may need some changes to fit your evolving circumstances.

This has been my own situation. I have been working at home for almost 20 years. During that time, my situation has changed several times as my family's health status has changed, and as my own needs and desires have shifted. This has made it necessary to adjust the strategies I use for getting things done in productive ways.

When I was still working in the corporate world, I often wished there was a way I could work at home part of the time or even full time. I wanted the option to set my own schedule and to enjoy the pleasure of being in my own home environment. I had a small business on the side, so I worked at home during some evenings and weekends. I liked having the variety of the job and the side business, but I wished that I could be at home more of the time.

One of my first forays into working at home was doing a job share with another colleague. Between us, we held one full time corporate job. During the half time when I wasn't at the job, I was completing much of my formal training as a coach. It was very similar to going to graduate school. I really enjoyed the extra time at home, but I missed the full-time income. When my colleague decided she wanted to go back to working full time, my choices were to go back to full time work, or to leave the job. At that time, I chose to return to full time employment, but I wished I could have found a way to work at home more.

About a year later, this employer did a series of layoffs. I knew this might be my opportunity to make the shift and to have some financial resources because of the layoff. That is in fact what happened. I was delighted to be able to finally have the option to work full time from home with my own business! But it also meant I would need to learn how to be productive with my time working at home as well as managing the household. But I was determined to jump in and do the best I could in the process. I did some things right and I made some mistakes along the way. I'm glad you'll be able to learn from my experience!

If you are already working from home, take a few minutes to think about your situation. What are you enjoying about it? What are the things you are able to do productively? Are there certain times of day when you feel more productive and energetic and other times of day when you have less energy and lower productivity? What challenges seem to get in the way of being productive as you work at home?

Take a look at your family's circumstances. Have there been recent changes in your family's situation, such as the ages or activities of your family members, or the health of one or more of your family members?

Taking a few minutes to think about these questions will be a strong first step in helping you to fine tune your methods and strategies for working at home productively.

If you aren't yet actually working at home, you may be thinking about the possibility. As you consider the option of working at home, what are you imagining it could be like? What are the positives you could see for yourself and your family? What are the challenges or concerns you might face? What steps have you taken so far, to work out the details of how you would work at home in a productive way?

A third possibility is you may have been working at home but now want or need to be out of the home more of the time. This may be because you need to pursue a job for the income or the benefits. It might be that you miss the interaction with other people in the work setting. Or it may be that, for some reason, your home isn't as viable a place for you to work anymore. There can be a number of reasons why you may want or need to be out of your house more often.

I found I reached a point after a few years of working at home where I needed and wanted to be out of the house and around other people more of the time. I didn't really want to pursue a regular job outside the home. So, at first, I would take a break and go run errands just to get out of the house, but this ended up using too much of my prime business time for tasks that weren't a high priority.

I shifted to focus more on business related things if I wanted to leave the house during the day. This included going to networking and professional association meetings, speaking for groups, and meeting some of my clients at their offices. I moved most of my errands or other personal activities to the end of the day or to the weekends. These out of the house activities take some planning and coordination, but they have helped me to enjoy a more satisfying activity mix in my schedule and to feel less "cooped up" in the house all day.

So, where are you now, as far as working at home goes? By taking a few minutes to take stock, you will be better able to choose the ideas and strategies in this book that may be the most helpful to you.

Could Working At Home Help You to Be More Productive?

The next great question to consider is whether working at home could help you to be more productive. Perhaps you have found, as I did, that working in corporate jobs often meant working in a fairly noisy environment with lots of potential interruptions and distractions. The work schedule is determined by the management team and may be earlier or later than you might choose yourself.

The projects are often a mix as far as your level of enjoyment or fulfillment goes. This is normal for most jobs. The other thing about working for someone else is your income is determined by other people. Your performance goals are also set by other people and the teams you work with are selected by other people as well.

You may find that you can be more productive working at home than in a traditional job. There are fewer meetings, more privacy, and more schedule flexibility. There are also more options to work in the ways that fit you best, whether it's in the early morning or later in the day, with sounds in the background, or not, taking frequent breaks or working late into the night. Having the freedom to set up your work schedule and environment to suit you are important parts of the strategy for maximizing your productivity when you work at home.

At the same time there are challenges that can stand in the way of being productive when you work at home. In fact, that may be the reason you are reading this book. There are always things that need to be done at home. This can include everything from the laundry to the dishes to errands to yard work. Depending on the business tasks you need to do and how excited you are about doing them, the distractions at home can be very enticing! On top of that, when you work for yourself, you don't have other people around you to help you stay on track and focused on your work tasks.

But the truth is, with some good strategies and a bit of experimentation, it is possible to be quite productive working at home. You have the opportunity to choose the place or places in your house where you will work. Or you can choose to be portable with your work and head out from the house to another location such as the library or a coffee shop where you can work. You can choose which tasks to focus on first and which to save for later. You can also choose when to take stretch breaks, and even set your own starting and quitting times.

When you are an entrepreneur working at home, you can choose the equipment you use, including the type of computer and printer and phone. You can choose what software to use, when to update it, and how you will handle things like backups. You can also choose how to grow your business, including how to market it, what types of clients to serve, which services and products you want to offer, and even your prices.

Having these choices available gives you a lot of room to customize your business and the way you work. In the chapters ahead, we'll cover a wide range of options to help you tailor methods and systems that will work well for you and will help you be productive in the process.

SECTION TWO

WHY PRODUCTIVITY IS A WORTHWHILE GOAL

In this section we'll explore some of the many reasons people work at home. This will lead us right into the reasons it's worthwhile to find ways to be productive in the process. There are many reasons people choose to work at home. Some of the most common are family reasons and health reasons. And a third reason is equally important and that is the freedom to pursue your own goals and dreams, both personal and professional. It's even possible you may have reasons which tie in with all three areas. As your life changes and evolves, you may find that each of these reasons is part of your motivation for working at home.

For myself, over the past 17 years that I've worked at home full time, all three of these reasons have come into play, sometimes at the same time. Initially my reason for working at home was to be able to pursue my business dreams. I wanted to have the freedom to design my work schedule and to have time for things like exercise and connecting with the important people in my life.

Think about the reasons you work at home, or that you would like to work at home. As you read through this section, additional ideas may occur to you. List all of the reasons large and small. With this list and some creative thought, you have an excellent chance of being able to design your at home work experience to meet many of your goals over time.

Chapter Three

Reasons People Choose
To Work at Home

Family Reasons

One of the most common reasons people choose to work at home is because of family situations. This can be related to having more time to be with your children or grandchildren. It could be that you have a spouse who is on the road a lot and managing the household while he or she is away is easier if you work from home. Or it may be that you have elderly family members who need more support and assistance. You will be in good company if one of your reasons for working at home is because of family circumstances.

In recent years, family reasons have been a big part of my reasons for continuing to work at home. After my parents retired, my mother's health began to decline, and they started needing more of my help. Eventually they reached the point where they decided to move to a senior community that would have the full range of levels of care, from independent living to dementia care to skilled nursing and even hospice care.

I knew they were going to need extra support and assistance with the move and beyond. Having the flexible structure available with working at home made it possible for me to offer more support than if I was still working in the full time corporate job where I was previously, especially with the frequent business travel that was part of the job.

One of my friends, Donna, has a son with special needs. Because her husband was in the military for many years, she chose to homeschool her son to provide him with a more consistent educational experience during the many moves the family made. By running her own business at home, Donna was able to accomplish this goal.

Even after her husband retired from the military, the rhythm of the household continued to work well with her working at home and assisting their son. A few years later an elderly relative needed to come to live with the family. Donna's family was able to accommodate this because she was working at home. Donna reconfigured the household needs so that she was still able to have time to run her business, and the other family members helped with keeping the household running well.

This friend is not unusual in her work at home situation. Over the course of several years, her work arrangements needed to change and evolve to meet her business needs as well as her family needs. She was able to work through these changes each time and in fact has become quite the expert at helping other families to work successfully at home. Now her husband also has a business of his own and works at home too.

Another friend, Jenny, enjoyed being a full-time mother when her children were young. She started her home-based business when her kids were in high school. She wanted to be able to be with them in the evenings, and to take time off if one of them was sick. By working at home, she was able to adjust her business schedule to match their school holidays and vacation days. Over the years, as her children graduated from high school and went off to college, she was able to continue to fine tune her schedule to align with theirs. This arrangement has given her the best of both worlds, time with her family as well as time to work on her business.

If you have a family and want the flexibility to have time with them, you may find that working at home is a good option for you. It will require persistence and creativity and determination to make it work well. But it can be done. You'll need to make adjustments as your family situation evolves, but the rewards of time with the people who are most precious to you can be well worth it!

Health Reasons

Another reason many people choose to work at home is related to health needs. It could be your own health situation, or the health needs of someone in your family. Working at home can provide flexibility to accommodate a wide variety of special health needs and changes. It can provide you with many options that aren't available in a traditional job.

Being able to address my own health needs is one of the benefits of working at home that I truly value. I have had migraine headaches for many years. It is not unusual for me to wake up with a migraine, with no prior warning. I'm so grateful that there are now medications that I can take if I have a migraine. The meds usually ease some of the pain of a migraine within a few hours, but it usually doesn't subside completely. By working at home, I can shift my work schedule, or focus on less mentally strenuous work on days when I don't feel well. Knowing I can make these adjustments gives me peace of mind.

Working at home may offer you some of these same advantages if you have health challenges. It can be easier to schedule and go to medical appointments or to pick up prescriptions or other needed items. You may find it easier to do any needed treatments or physical therapy exercises when you are at home. This kind of flexibility can feel encouraging and help you to maintain your optimism which helps to support your health and wellbeing too.

If you have days or hours when you are not feeling as well as you would like, working at home can offer you more flexibility to schedule in periods of rest or even a nap if you need it. One of my colleagues has an ongoing health condition which can flare up unexpectedly. On days when this happens, she starts her day with a specific slower routine and builds in time for treatments that can help to ease her discomfort. She often takes a short afternoon nap on these days which helps her to feel well enough to get some work done afterwards.

This points to an excellent strategy which I'll describe in more detail in a later chapter. The main idea is to plan, as my colleague has, to have a strategy for handling days when she doesn't feel well. She can shift into a "Plan B" type of schedule that includes actions and resources she has thought about ahead of time, knowing there will be days when she needs to use them. You may be able to follow a similar strategy. With some planning, you will be better prepared to handle days when you may not feel your best, and still be able to get some work done on these days.

It may be that the health needs you need to accommodate are not your own health challenges. If you have a family member with health issues that you need to be able to assist with, working at home may give you some extra flexibility to accommodate these needs and to fit your work in and around them.

As I mentioned earlier, as my mother's health declined there were more situations when my help was needed. This included some routine things like helping to get her to medical appointments when she could no longer drive. Fortunately, these kinds of appointments could usually be scheduled in advance which made it easier to plan for work tasks too.

My mother also had some medical emergencies that required trips to the emergency room and subsequent hospitalizations. These types of challenges happen unexpectedly and need an immediate response. Mom's hospital stays lasted several days and meant I spent many hours in her room. I was grateful I was able to take a tote bag with my laptop computer and get some work done when she was resting or sleeping.

You may find as I have that personal or family health needs can change over time. It can be a blessing to be able to adapt and adjust to meet those needs and still be able to fit your work around them. I was especially glad I could help my mother with her health needs in the final months of her life. If you or one of your family members has health needs, you may find that working at home is a very helpful option for you.

Opportunities to Pursue Multiple Interests

A big reason many people like to work at home is the freedom to design their own life and schedule. This can also include the opportunity to pursue a variety of business goals, and perhaps even more than one business.

One of the most important reasons I wanted to work from home was to have the flexibility to create a work schedule that fit my own best style. For me this includes working later in the day rather than in the early morning. I also like to take a break in the afternoon to do some non-work activities and then do more work later in the evening. Working at home offers this kind of flexibility.

Another reason people like to work at home is to have the option to travel or to pursue other personal interests. One of my clients, Vicki, has several relatives who live in another country. By working from home, she can to travel to visit these family members several times a year without having to ask a boss for time off or worrying if she has enough vacation time.

Perhaps you have a strong desire to be involved in community or volunteer activities. Working at home can give you flexibility to arrange your schedule to accomplish this goal. One of the things I have done several times is to offer a few pro bono coaching sessions to nonprofit leaders as a way to support their organizations. By having flexibility I've been able to fit this into my schedule in a way that worked well.

You may have a goal of returning to school for some additional education or training. When you work at home, you may find that you can work your classes and your study time into your schedule along with your work activities. This can be especially helpful if you need to attend classes in person, but it is helpful for online classes too.

One of my clients, Ann, had a dream of being able to complete her college degree while still running her business. Because her business was home-based, she had the flexibility to set her appointments and client work around her class schedule, even as it changed from semester to semester. She was able to complete her degree and has gone on to new levels of success with her at-home business.

Working at home can give you flexibility between regular jobs too. One of my friends, Terri, had been laid off several times from corporate jobs. Her mother was also getting older and needed more support. Terri decided to take a series of temp jobs and to work at home between these engagements. This gave her more options and flexibility. She was able to defer taking assignments during times when her mother needed extra care. This combination of options gave Terri the extra flexibility she needed during that season of her life.

You may be a creative person who likes to have the flexibility to have more than one business venture. Working at home gives you a lot of freedom for this possibility. Tonya is this type of creative person. She thrives on having multiple businesses, and she is always thinking of new possibilities. Because she works at home, she can divide her time among several different ventures. Two of her businesses are very busy in the fall season. Another one is more active during the spring and summer. She has even started a couple of new ventures and then sold the businesses and the related materials so that she could profit from the sale and then turn her attention to fresh ideas.

You may have a spouse or a partner who travels a great deal with their work. It can often be easier to manage the household and take care of appointments for the house and the family if you are able to work at home. I have also seen this work if the person working at home wants to travel with their spouse some of the time. Working from home can make this possible.

As you can see, there are many reasons why people may prefer to work at home. It allows them to express themselves and to pursue passions and interests in addition to their business. Having multiple interests is a great reason to be as productive as possible with your business. Take a few minutes with your notebook and capture the reasons why you would like to work from home, or why you may already have made this choice. Writing down all of your reasons can help to clarify your motivations for finding great ways to be productive with your at-home business.

Chapter Four

What Do You Hope to Accomplish By Working at Home?

Let Yourself Dream

When you have identified your reasons for working at home, it can help to boost your motivation. Even if not all the reasons are things you are thrilled about, such as challenging health circumstances, it helps to be honest with yourself about it. Go a step further and let yourself think about what positive things could be possible if you approached it from a dreaming and designing perspective.

What I mean by this is, rather than just accepting how things are now by default, you can put your own style and preferences into your work plan and approach. The more it reflects your tastes and needs the more energizing and engaging it can be for you. This can open the way to strong productivity too.

I especially want to encourage you to do this if you've been working at home for quite a while. Taking a fresh look now will help you see adjustments that will feel good and work better for you. Even if you are only able to activate a few of the things you dream about, it can improve the quality of your everyday life.

This is a good time to use your notebook to capture your thoughts as you consider the following questions. Let yourself imagine some answers that would feel really good to you!

A good place to start is by thinking about the times of day you focus on your work tasks. If you are a morning person, are you actually using a good part of most mornings to do focused work? Along those same lines, if you are more of an afternoon person or a night owl, do your work times fit your higher energy times, or are you trying to fit into a "morning person" schedule?

Think about what it could look like if you were really productive as you are working at home. Imagine the kinds of things you would be able to get done each day. Think about the amount of work that would feel good to accomplish each day, realistically. Visualize yourself making progress toward your three main projects or key goals for the next 90 days.

What are the things you like about your current work area at home? What are the aspects of your work area that you aren't as pleased with? Is there a good amount of light? Is there enough space for your computer or your materials and equipment? How is the noise level? Too noisy? Too quiet? How is the seating in your work area? Comfortable, or maybe not as comfortable as you would like?

Take inventory of your computer, phone, and other technology and equipment. Is it reasonably functional and up to date? Or not as current or as functional as you would like or as you really need to do your best work? What are a couple of things that would most benefit from an update, if it was possible?

Now consider your network of people, your colleagues and your support team. In your business, you may be "wearing all of the hats" even though some of the roles and tasks aren't the best fit for your skills and preferences. Do you have some part time or contract support team members like an accountant, a tech person, an assistant, a web person, a mentor?

Look at your opportunities for getting out of the house occasionally. This can be for personal or for business reasons. Do you have a professional group you belong to? Are you able to participate in some activities in your community such as volunteer, church or exercise activities?

How are you doing with taking good care of yourself physically at home? This can include everything from getting enough good quality sleep, eating in a fairly healthy way, exercising, and getting some fresh air outside. Are you taking regular breaks to refresh and reenergize yourself? And are you taking some vacation time off regularly, even if it's just long weekends?

Aim to Make it Truly Fit Your Needs

By answering the questions above, you can see the positive aspects you already have in place. You can also see some areas where you might like to make changes. For each of these things, let yourself think about what you would like instead.

Try doing this in your notebook using a two-column format. Write the aspects you are not as pleased about on the left side. Then on the right side of the page, for each item, write out your thoughts about what you would like instead. After you have written out these ideas, choose two or three changes that you might want to implement.

Another way to approach this is to use the "Stop, Start, Continue" method. This is an easy, yet powerful way to begin to identify changes you might want to consider.

The first thing to identify are things you want or need to stop doing. For example, one of the things I have stopped doing is answering my home telephone during my main work hours. If I was away from home at a traditional job, I wouldn't be there to answer, and voicemail would take the call. I decided to do the same thing when I am working at home. However, I find that hearing the phone ring is distracting and it can be tempting to look at the caller ID to see who is calling. I have gone a step further and now I turn off the ring sounds during my main work hours. When calls come in, they still go to voicemail, but I don't hear the ringing and risk the distraction from getting productive work done. I check for messages in the middle of the day and again around 4:30. This enables me to return calls, if needed, before 5 p.m.

Along the same lines, I turn off the ringer for my mobile phone while I am working. It's just too distracting to be interrupted by a phone call while I am trying to concentrate on work tasks. And, as with my home phone, I check for messages at midday and toward the end of the day, so I can return calls if needed. I also adjusted the settings for a few key people who might have emergency calls I need to take so those calls will still come through. You can do something similar with your phone if you find it is a distraction that keeps you from getting your most productive work done.

Under the "Start" category, think about strategies you want to begin doing to improve your work setting or habits. In the upcoming chapters in this book, I'll be sharing many ideas that could go on your "Start" list.

As an example of a recent thing I have started doing and that I have found very helpful, is doing my end of the day action review in a spiral notebook. On the left, I make a quick list of the work-related tasks I focused on that day. On the right, I jot down the personal things I did that day. It takes about five minutes to complete.

Keeping these two ongoing lists helps me to see I am making progress, that I worked on some tasks that were important to me, and that I got some personal things done too. It also helps me to see trends over time. I can see if I am focusing on the work tasks I really want to be doing, or if I have gone several days without working on something and have fallen into a procrastination pattern. I can see which personal tasks may actually be things I am doing as a way of avoiding a work task that feels like it may be hard or unpleasant.

In the category of "Continue," these are strategies or tasks you are doing already and which you think would be beneficial to continue doing. There are two subcategories that I like to suggest for this. One is "Do More" and the other is "Do Less." As you might guess, these are things you want to continue doing but which might benefit from increasing or decreasing a bit.

An example of "Do Less" might be how often you check your email. It's important to check your email but if you are doing it too often, or if you are being interrupted by email notifications, it may be undermining your productivity. The "Do Less" strategy might look like choosing just two or three times during the day to check your email, such as 10 a.m., 1:00 p.m. and 4:00 p.m. This still gives you time to respond to urgent email items and yet it protects your time in between so you can stay focused and productive.

A "Do More" item might be to make a point to reach out to three or four people each day instead of doing this only occasionally. This will strengthen your business network and can support your business success.

Take a few minutes now to make your own Start, Stop, Continue lists. Include some "Do More" and "Do Less" in the Continue category. Keep these lists so you can continue to add to them, or to check items off as you implement them. Review your lists every 90 days to see your progress and to update your lists. This simple strategy is a great way to keep an ongoing focus on ideas and strategies to customize your work space and to enhance your productivity.

SECTION THREE

WHAT IF YOU COULD DESIGN YOUR WORK AT HOME EXPERIENCE TO MAXIMIZE YOUR PRODUCTIVITY?

In this section, we'll dive deeper into a wide range of techniques and strategies that can really help you to increase your productivity. As you read it, keep your notebook nearby so you can capture the ideas you think will work best for you. Even if you are not sure if an idea will work for you, capture it anyway and add it to your list. This will help you remember it and to consider it again later.

Your work at home arrangements will naturally shift and change over time as your life and business change and evolve. Every time your situation changes, you will need to make small or large changes in the way you work. Keeping a list of great strategies ready and waiting in the wings makes it faster and easier to make the adjustments and builds your confidence that you have a collection of ideas you can quickly tap into, rather than having to start from scratch each time.

In this section I'll get you started with a good collection of strategies from my own experience, as well as the ideas from my clients and colleagues. There is no need to struggle to come up with your own techniques unless you enjoy being creative and unique. If that is the case, I strongly encourage you to go for it because it will provide joy and pleasure that will energize you.

Chapter Five

Creating Your Work Space At Home

Your Workspace

Your workspace has a huge influence on your productivity. A great thing about working at home is you have a lot of choices and options for designing or adjusting your workspace to really suit your needs. Let's talk about how to approach this, with productivity in mind.

Start to think about the various places in your home where you could work. You may want to choose more than one area. For example, if you have an extra room or an extra bedroom, that can give you a nice amount of space for your home office. Even if you use this room for other purposes in addition to your business, a separate room can give you more control over the light and sounds. It can help to limit interruptions too.

Perhaps you don't have a separate room, or perhaps you don't want to be in a room away from the main part of the house. There are plenty of other options. Look at the other parts of your house or apartment with a creative eye for places where you could work.

For example, many people like to work at the kitchen table. You'll need to work around meal times, but this can be a good option if you won't be interrupted by other people in the household. It may be that other members are away from home during the day and you can use the kitchen table during this time. Some kitchens have a built-in alcove or desk surface that may also serve as a good work space for you.

In a similar way, you may be able to put a desk or a table in the corner of another room in your house and use that as a workspace. I have a table I've placed in the corner of the living area of my house. I use this as a desk, especially when I want to be able to look out the window or when I am on a video call. It has good natural light and a neutral background for the video camera. My husband also likes this table and he often uses it as a work area on the weekends. Do you have a corner in a room where you could place a table to create a workspace like this?

Perhaps you like to have the option to relax in a comfortable chair or on the sofa, or even sitting up in your bed. You can use these comfy places as a work space, even if it isn't your main work area. You may find it helpful to use a lap desk with a pillow underneath to give you a flat surface for your laptop computer.

If the weather is pleasant during some seasons of the year, you may want to use an area on your balcony or in your backyard as an occasional work area. In the spring and fall, there is mild weather where I live. I really enjoy working outside, especially when I am writing or doing paperwork tasks. I use a folding table and chair that I can carry outside, and I place them wherever the shade is.

Think about where you can store your business materials and equipment. You may have a shelf or a closet with some space where you can store items. A file cabinet tucked away in a corner can be very useful. If you have the space, I have found that having a tall, 5-drawer lateral file cabinet is great for storing a wide variety of business files and materials. You can often purchase a used commercial grade file cabinet at a local office furniture outlet store. A bookcase is another practical item. You can use it to store not only books but also equipment or papers or boxes of smaller items.

As you can see there are a variety of places where you can work at home. Experiment with several of these options to see which ones will work best for you.

Portable Options

In addition to identifying places at home where you can work, look for ways to make some of your business activities portable. Depending on the nature of your business, not everything will be easy to make portable. I encourage you to be creative and think of at least one or two of your regular work tasks that can be done on a portable basis.

By portable, I mean you could pack up the necessary materials into a tote bag or a rolling laptop bag and take them with you. Identify tasks that can be done with your phone or iPad, or with a simple tablet of paper and a pen. The goal is to make it easy for you to be able to work at more than one location, whether it's in your home or away from home. With the wonderful advances in technology that are readily available, it's easier than ever to take some of your work with you wherever you go. You'll find that being portable opens up some additional productivity strategies as you'll discover in the next few chapters.

Think about which of your work-related tasks could possibly be made portable. Writing is an excellent example. Whether you like to work on a laptop or on your phone or with a tablet and pen, writing can be very portable. Thinking and planning can also be done in many places. Some types of paperwork as well as reading can be very portable. Learning can be done in many places as online courses can be accessed anywhere you have an internet connection. Even phone calls can be done in a portable way, as long as you have a quiet place where you can hear and where you won't disturb other people.

Out of the House Options

As you are thinking about places where you can work at home, remember to think about places outside of your house too. This may sound contradictory, especially since this book is about working at home. But being a home-based entrepreneur can, and perhaps should, include options for working away from your house too.

This can include things like attending conferences, meeting with clients at their locations, going to networking events and professional meetings, or just going to a place away from your home to work for a few hours. I encourage you to include several of these options in your Productivity Plan.

In your notebook, start a list of places where you could work away from your house. This can include the library, coffee shops, cafes, and coworking spaces. You may even have a colleague who would enjoy meeting up with you at one of these locations, so you can visit for a few minutes as well as get some work done.

There are several reasons why this strategy can help you be productive. It provides some variety in your schedule. This can be energizing and it can also spark creative ideas. Getting out of your home also brings you into contact with other people. The trick is to find the right mix of at home and away from home work activities.

Some of this is influenced by your personality and individual preferences. If you are an introvert, you are likely more energized by "alone time" and a quieter environment. You'll probably prefer a smaller amount of outside activities and you'll likely prefer contact with people you already know and feel comfortable with. On the other hand, if you are an extrovert who is energized by being around other people, you may need more people contact, perhaps much more, to be at your best.

Whichever style is more like you, use this knowledge about yourself to choose and design your away from home work locations and activities so they help you stay energized and productive.

Chapter Six

Tools and Equipment to Boost Your Productivity

Furniture and Equipment

In Chapter Five we explored the variety of places you could work at home. We also began to explore what it might take to make some of your work tasks portable, so you could do them from a variety of locations if you want to or need to.

In this chapter, we'll go a step further and explore some of the tools and equipment that can help to boost and sustain high productivity. Some of these may be items you already have available. Others may be new options for you to consider. I encourage you to take stock of what you are already using and what you have at home already. Start with these items but be willing and open to trying some different things that may make a big difference in your work life.

Furniture and larger pieces of equipment are often the first things we think of when we think about work arrangements. You don't need a traditional desk to be productive with your home-based business. There are a wide variety of work surfaces that may meet your needs. Be willing to rethink your options to see which will work best for you now.

One of the easiest options is a table of some type. I use a table which is about 3 feet by 4 feet in size. It was probably originally intended to be a nice modern wooden kitchen table. It has two wings or leaves that can expand the table to double its original size, if needed. It doesn't have drawers like a traditional desk would, so I use a file cabinet and a bookcase to meet some of my storage needs.

Some people use a dining room table, especially if their work involves large drawings or working with materials or fabrics or other large size items. In my extra bedroom I have a modular arrangement that came from a retail organizing store. My arrangement is made of wood and has shelves for my large collection of books and it also has room for my printer and extra reams of printer paper. A part of the framework is a large flat piece of wood that is about 30 inches by 60 inches. One end of this flat piece of wood rests on a shelf and the other end has two legs which makes it into a table or desk type surface.

There are times when I like to stand and work, to let my body be in a different position after sitting for a while. The island in my kitchen is a good height for this, so I often work there with my laptop and a cup of tea. I have also found it is wise to wear shoes with good support rather than standing barefoot on the hard floor, especially if you are going to be working there for more than a few minutes.

You can also find tall cafe style tables at retail or outlet stores. These tall tables along with a comfortable tall chair can let you sit or stand and it can be a nice alternative work area.

On a smaller scale, you can use a coffee table (while seated on a large floor pillow), a pillow top desk that fits on your lap, or even a TV tray or a folding table or a clipboard for a work surface. I use all of these kinds of surfaces at various times, especially when I want to work somewhere different for a change of pace. All but the coffee table can be easily folded or tucked away when they are not in use.

If you look around your home, you may already have some items like these which you can use as work surfaces. These

48

types of items are also fairly inexpensive to purchase at retail stores or discount outlet stores.

For other furniture items, consider a filing cabinet and some shelves. These items come in a variety of sizes, colors and styles. You can purchase very nice coordinated items, or you can find inexpensive secondhand items if you are just getting started or want to keep your expenses as low as possible.

Another important item to consider is the type of chair you use. You can find a wide range of office chairs now, from the plain to the very high tech, from low cost or secondhand to top of the line. At the very least, I encourage you to choose a chair that makes it easy to sit up straight and that offers good back support. You may find that a straight back dining table chair will work well. When your body has good support it helps you to stay energized and productive. If your chair is uncomfortable, you may feel like avoiding it and avoiding your work. I'm not against relaxing in an armchair or a sofa occasionally with my laptop or my iPad to do some work, but I wouldn't suggest it as your primary work arrangement.

Finally, be sure you have good lighting for your work areas. This can include natural light from a window during the day as well as a table lamp or floor lamp to enable you to work early in the morning or later in the evening. Consider the color of the bulb you use. There are now many good options to choose from. If possible, go to a store that has a variety of light bulbs available and that has a display to show you the different "colors" of white light bulbs that are available. I personally like bulbs that are similar to natural daylight, but you can also find bulbs that are a "cooler" white or a "warmer" white too. Encourage you to experiment to see which is best for you.

Electronics and Small Tools

In addition to your computer and your phone, there are a number of electronics and small tools that can be very helpful in your quest for a productive work environment. For example, a printer is an important item for your work at home. You can choose from inkjet or laser printer styles and there are many good ones on the market now. Consider a wireless printer so you can print from anywhere you happen to be working in your home. Keep extra printer paper and extra toner or ink cartridges on hand so you never have to interrupt your productive workflow to get more supplies.

It is also smart to consider having one or even two extra sets of chargers for your electronic devices. This includes not only the cords to plug into electrical outlets but also small portable chargers you can carry with you when you are working away from your home.

Another useful item is an extension cord. Tuck one into your tote bag to carry along with your laptop. This can enable you to plug your laptop into an electrical outlet even if you aren't able to sit very close to the outlet. It can make a big difference in being able to keep your equipment charged up and working for several hours when you are working away from home.

A larger battery backup/reserve power source is useful if you live in an area that is subject to frequent power outages. This piece of equipment is not inexpensive, but it can give you time to back up your work or even to work for an extra few minutes if necessary during a power outage.

Other types of equipment that you may want to consider are a shredder, an electric hole puncher, and an electric label maker. A headset or an earpiece is helpful for conference calls or video conferences.

It can also be helpful to have easy access to office supplies you use most often such as pens, paperclips, a stapler, file folders, tablets, and scissors. Because I work in several parts of my house, I keep a few of these basic items near the two or three main areas where I work. I've found it to be a great convenience and a timesaver to have them close at hand rather than have to walk to another room for a needed item.

For comfort, you may also enjoy having a fan to keep you cool on warm days and a lap blanket or a sweater for cool days. If you enjoy drinking coffee or tea while you work, consider getting a good coffeemaker or a kettle to make it quick and easy to make. If you like to listen to music while you work, a nice quality speaker or two may be a nice addition to your work area.

There may be other types of tools and electronics that are useful. Talk with other entrepreneurs about the tools and resources that they find most helpful. There are always new products and services being developed that can help you to get your work done well and that can increase your productivity too.

Online Tools

Online resources of all kinds are available to help you with business productivity and success. New online tools and apps are being developed constantly. Here are a few that you may find helpful.

Use your smartphone's voicemail system to capture messages rather than allowing the phone to interrupt you throughout the day. Create a pleasant professional outgoing message that communicates a bit about you and your business rather than just using the default generic message. When making phone calls, cluster or batch them together by making your calls one right after the other. Your phone can also be used for video style calls or conference calls, allowing you to see the other people you are talking with and to be seen by them. It's helpful to use a headset or earbud for best sound quality.

Consider apps and programs that let you track your actions, make checklists, time your focused work tasks as well as your breaks, and help complete tasks that are important to you. The goal is to use tools and apps that truly help you and not to get bogged down with so many that they get in the way of your effectiveness. It's a judgment call that has to be made over and over as new resources become available.

Here are some online resources I find helpful as of 2018. Carbonite is great for backing up computer files automatically on a regular basis. Dropbox is good for saving computer files to the cloud and for being able to access them from any of my devices, anywhere I can access the internet. This has proven to be very helpful for productivity on the go and for sharing files with other people. The Notes app on my iPhone is great for all types of notes. I use it for lists of library books I may want to check out, travel ideas, writing parts of this book when I am out away from home, and ideas for business projects. I also use the apps for social media to search for people on LinkedIn and to tune in to Facebook Live broadcasts.

The timer in the clock app is great for timing my work on focused tasks and to give me a five-minute warning before phone calls or webinars are scheduled to start. The local library also has an app I use almost daily to request books and renew books that may be helpful in my business. YouTube and Google and Amazon are all excellent for online business research to learn and to gather information for business projects.

Take a few minutes now to take stock of the furniture and equipment and online tools you already use. Make a wish list of additional items that could be helpful to you. There is usually no need to rush out and purchase things immediately. Use the items you already have and as your business income grows, you may want to add some of the items on your wish list.

Even though the furniture and equipment and online resources you use in your business are a very important part of setting up your business to be successful, they alone cannot make your business succeed. Ultimately, it is your prioritized actions and habits that have the biggest influence on your business success. In upcoming chapters, I'll cover a wide variety of action strategies to help you in these areas.

Chapter Seven

Staying Energized and Healthy to Boost Your Productivity

Be Proactive

One of the great benefits of working at home is that you have a lot of freedom to arrange your work schedule to fit your energy and health needs. This can range from taking care of your own health challenges, to helping other family members with their health needs, to building in time to maintain and enhance your health. I strongly encourage you to be very proactive in addressing these needs.

Being proactive starts with great self-care, taking steps to protect and enhance your health. When I coach my clients, I encourage them to address six foundational steps that can make a positive difference in their wellbeing. As you read about each one, think about ways you may be able to work some or all of them into your work at home arrangements.

First, aim to get a good amount of high quality sleep most nights. One of the first things I did when I shifted to working at home was to adjust my sleep schedule. When I worked in the corporate world it wasn't unusual for me to get only four to six hours of sleep each night. Working at home gave me the opportunity to get at least six hours a night, and seven or eight hours whenever possible.

I also made some changes to my sleep environment, making it darker at night and making it quieter. When my husband and I adopted a new cat, we made the decision right from the start to have him sleep outside the bedroom so his movements during the night would not disturb our sleep. These changes have really helped to improve our sleep quality. Take some steps to improve your sleep quality and your sleep environment in whatever way you can.

The second key area is to be proactive about your food and water intake. Working at home almost always gives you more choices and flexibility about what you eat, how it is prepared, and when you eat. I encourage you to drink plenty of water. An easy way to do this is to fill a water container with ice and water in the morning so you can drink water throughout the day.

Think about your easiest breakfast options. You may prefer a hearty breakfast or just something light. I'm not usually very hungry in the morning, but I know there is value to fueling my body at the start of my day. My solution to this is often a quick protein smoothie, so I can just drink my breakfast. If I'm heading out the door for an appointment, I may take a protein bar with me instead, because it is quick and easy.

For lunch, you may want to aim for quick and simple but nourishing meals. This may be leftovers from dinner the night before or it may be a hearty bowl of soup. Make a list of ideas for your morning and midday meals. Write them down so you don't have to take much time to decide what to eat. When you shop for food, stock your fridge and freezer and cupboards with ingredients that will make it easy for you to have breakfasts and lunches for the entire week.

The third core proactive choice is to get some physical movement during your day. This can be as simple as five minutes of movement every hour or taking 15 to 30 minutes during the day for some type of physical activity. Working at home gives you a lot of freedom to do this. You'll want to choose options that you and your health care provider feel are right for your needs.

I've tried a wide mix of activities over the years. One of my favorites right now are using a recumbent bike for a few minutes. I've found I can even read a book while I pedal, which is an extra bonus. Sometimes I just walk up and down the stairs in my house a few times.

I also have a few dumbbells that let me do a simple upper body strength training routine that a trainer helped to tailor for my needs. I recently purchased an inexpensive exercise mat that lets me do some simple floor exercises too. I like to take a walk in the evening with my husband or with a friend at least once a week.

The fourth core practice may be one of the simplest, yet most important ones. It is to go outside for a few minutes every day to get some fresh air. If you can get a few minutes of sunshine that is also great. There is something very restorative about going outside. Plan the timing for this to fit into your work schedule. You can use it as a short work break, or you may even have a good place at home where you can sit outside and do a work task, such as at a table in your back yard.

The fifth core practice is to have some type of contact with people every day. This can be as simple as talking with the sales person who helps you when you are doing an errand, it might be calling a friend or colleague to check in with a quick phone call. It could be walking with a friend in the evening, which can combine three core things at once: fresh air, people contact, and physical movement. If you have more physical limitations, put technology to work and use your phone or a videoconferencing app to connect with a friend or colleague for at least a few minutes every day.

The sixth core practice is to do something every day that gives you a sense of fun or pleasure or joy. As with the other core practices, start with simple options to make it easy to do. This could be petting your cat or dog, reading a book by a favorite author, watching a funny video, buying yourself flowers, wearing your favorite color, sipping your favorite coffee or tea, or watching the sunrise or the sunset. The idea is to be intentional about it and to deliberately weave these enjoyable activities into your day. They will lift your spirits!

Work It into Your Productivity Plan

The six core practices all sound good in theory. The challenge comes with finding time to do them, especially when you are busy with your work and with personal responsibilities. The answer is to work them into your Productivity Plan, as part of your day. In this section I'll talk about some ways to do this.

One of the basic principles of productivity is to alternate work activities and "rest" activities. I put "rest" in quotes because it may literally be to rest and take a break, but it can also just be a different type of task that will refresh and reenergize you. For example, if you are focused on writing, you are most likely sitting at a computer or at a table with paper and pen. It is primarily a mental task where you are coming up with the words to write to express your thoughts. In contrast, if you are at a networking meeting, you are probably standing and talking with another person, perhaps with some food or drink in your hand. This takes a completely different type of energy than the writing task. Now think about the task of skimming through your email messages or listening to your voicemail messages. These are often very routine straightforward tasks.

A great strategy for being productive and keeping your energy going is to rotate among different types of tasks like these, rather than spending several hours at a time on just one of them. You may need to experiment to find the length of time that will work best for you and even use a timer to help you remember to switch tasks as you get used to this method.

One of my favorite ways to use this productivity technique is to use 20-minute chunks. To make this work well, I set three timers, one for 20 minutes, one for 40 minutes and one for 60 minutes. For the first 20-minute chunk I work on a business task that is a high priority task. When the timer goes off, I switch to a different business task, specifically one that has a different feel or energy requirement, perhaps even something simple and routine. When the second 20 minutes is up, I switch to something that isn't work related at all. This might be one of the six core personal care activities such as going outside for fresh air or getting a snack and some water or even resting for 20 minutes. The secret is to use the timer and to switch after 20 minutes back to a focused work task.

You may find you can repeat the three 20-minute cycles for several hours and my energy stays pretty strong. You can plug in various work tasks, and different types of personal activities for the third 20-minute segment. The pattern is the same: two different work-related tasks followed by a personal activity, always "delegating" to the timer the task of keeping track of the time and keeping me on track with the process.

This method works especially well when you have a difficult or unpleasant but necessary work task. Breaking it into 20-minute chunks can help you to relax and realize you only have to work on it for 20 minutes at a time. Then you can switch to a less challenging work task that still gives you a sense of progress and accomplishment. And, perhaps even more importantly, it gives you the positive anticipation of a more pleasant or relaxing or reenergizing personal activity happening within the hour. It is amazing what a difference this can make for your frame of mind!

To be successful with the method, do a bit of preplanning. Make a list of tasks that can be part of the work related 20-minute chunks and a list of activities that can be part of the 20-minute rest and relax time. This is one of the keys to success because you want to be able to make the switch between tasks quickly, without much thought or internal debate about what your next activity will be. Have your materials ready to go so you can shift gears smoothly and quickly.

After you have tried this method a few times, you may want to modify it by stretching the times out a little bit. You may want to try 30 or even 45-minute work segments instead of 20 minutes. I encourage you not to stretch beyond 45 minutes or 50 minutes before you switch to a personal activity. My other suggestion is that you keep the personal activity to 20 minutes and resist the urge to make it shorter. Your brain and your body will benefit from the regular times of refreshment and you will be able to sustain your energy and focus for more hours of work during the day if you will allow yourself these rest or refreshing times.

You can also use these personal time chunks for some of the six core self-care activities. You many not fit all six into your work time each day. Some may fit better before or after your work day.

The other activities you may want to fit into one of two of the personal time chunks is a household task or two, especially something that is a bit active like straightening up some part of the house or watering the plants or switching out the laundry. But don't fall into the trap of using all of the personal time chunks for this type of household work activity or it can come to feel like a drudgery rather than the pleasant change of pace and the energy shift that it is meant to be.

To get started with this technique, take your notebook or journal and begin to make those two lists of possible activities. Divide the page into two columns. In the column on the left, make a list of work tasks that need to be done at this time. In the column on the right, make a list of activities that could be part of your personal 20-minute time chunks. Look back at the six core self-care activities for ideas. And don't be afraid to put some other things on your list like watching half of a favorite TV show you have recorded or reading for 20 minutes in the bestselling novel you are enjoying!

Workspace Elements

There are a variety of things you can do with your workspace to help yourself stay energized and productive. Many are fairly inexpensive too. Think about what could be added or removed or adjusted to better meet your current needs and style of working. I will share more possibilities to stimulate your thoughts.

See if one of the work areas in your home has a source of natural light and a view of the outdoors. I don't know of specific studies, but I know for myself, I feel more energized and connected to the real world when I work in an area where I have a view. I especially like being able to see the sky and something green like the trees, shrubs, or flowers.

If you don't have a window like this in your house that can be part of your workspace, consider finding a workspace outside of your house that has this type of view. Check out your local library branches and the coffeeshops in your area for starters. You may find you want a work space with fewer distractions for some tasks, but I encourage you to allow yourself to have some work areas that give you a view of nature too. These areas can provide a lift for your spirit.

Consider getting a pair of amber glasses to wear when you are using your computer or your phone at night. I recently found a pair which fit over the regular glasses I wear. There are also amber colored screens you can place over the computer screen. The amber color helps to reduce the amount of blue spectrum light you get at night which can help with sleep quality. If you wear prescription glasses, ask your optician about lenses that can help reduce blue light too.

Your indoor air quality is also something you can influence in positive ways when you work at home. Replacing your heating and air conditioning filter regularly makes a difference. I like to have a couple of fans in the house that have an ionizing setting to help keep the air clean and refreshed. It is also possible now to buy small, portable, room-size HEPA air filters. If you have allergies or if there are air quality issues in your area at certain times of year, you may find it beneficial to consider one of these units in your work area.

Think about comfort in your workspace too. I live in a hot climate and in the summer, I don't want to turn the thermostat down really low and try to make the whole house very cool. I set it a few degrees warmer and I turn on a fan in the area where I am working. Just feeling the cool area moving around me gives me the feeling of being cooler and that helps me to relax and be more productive than if I was stressing out about feeling hot and uncomfortable. Like so many things in this chapter, it is a simple thing, but it really makes a difference every day when I am working at home.

When the weather turns chilly, you may like to have a cup of something warm like coffee or tea. Wearing a favorite sweater or putting a soft fleece blanket over your legs can also add a welcome layer of warmth and comfort.

Think about putting something like a piece of art, a photograph, a greeting card from a friend, or a favorite mug with pens in your workspace. This is a bit of esthetic pleasure that makes you feel good every time you look at it. You can even have a little rotating "gallery" of items, or seasonal items that change throughout the year I like to put a couple of holiday items in my work area in the winter and something springy or summery during those seasons of the year.

Each of the strategies in this section is about ways to personalize and humanize your workspace. There is no need to work in the sterile work environment that may have been your experience in the corporate world! Enjoy creating your workspace to uniquely suit your style and your preferences! Make it a space you enjoy spending time in and you are more likely to look forward to being there each day.

Chapter Eight

Create Your Team

Tasks Other People Can Do

When you are planning your work and setting up your daily and weekly schedule I want you to think about the people who are on your team and how they can boost your productivity.

As an entrepreneur who works at home, you may be used to doing most of the tasks in your business yourself. But I want to broaden your thinking to include a variety of people who can play a vital role in supporting your business and multiplying your productivity. And, as with the other elements we have been talking about, I encourage you to think about this topic creatively and from a fresh perspective.

It can be easy to hold the belief that you need to be the person doing most or all of the work. This is a common thought, especially if you have built your business on a shoestring, keeping your expenses as low as possible.

It's easy to think to yourself, "I can do that task," rather than thinking instead about "who might be able to help me with this task?" It's easy to just keep doing the task, even if you don't especially enjoy doing it, or if you are not particularly expert with the task.

See which tasks in your business may fall into this pattern. Look for tasks you have been doing but which you might like to have someone else do, if possible. Make a list of these tasks in your notebook, thinking of them as candidates for a fresh approach. Then take a few minutes and rate each task. On a scale of 1 to 5, answer the following questions:

- How much do you enjoy doing this task?
- How well are you able to do this task?
- How essential is this task to your business success?
- Is it possible that someone else, with some training, could do some of this task?
- How much of a relief would it be to you to have help with this task?

Then ask yourself another important question: If you didn't have to do this task yourself every time, what other high value business tasks could you use this time and energy for? The answer to this question is extremely important. It is the "opportunity cost" question. By doing this task yourself, what other tasks are going undone or getting postponed?

As entrepreneurs, most of us have a long list of projects and business ideas we would like to be able to get to. Thinking about these questions can help you move to the next level in your business and pave the way for you to start some of those projects on your list.

Apply this same thought process to your household responsibilities too. Are you trying to do a lot of the household tasks yourself? Do you end up doing them just because you feel you can do them faster or easier or more "correctly" than someone else? The time and energy you devote to household tasks can also impact the time and energy available for your business.

In your notebook, make a list of household tasks that could just possibly be delegated or hired out, even if only occasionally at first. Putting them on the list doesn't mean you must immediately find someone else to do them. But it may help you to begin to think about the possibilities, and that is a great start!

Here are a few examples to consider: many types of household cleaning tasks, laundry, yard work, auto care, shredding, phone calls, errands, grocery shopping, and meal preparation. I am not saying you should delegate all of these tasks. I just want you to consider that some of these tasks can potentially completed by other people besides you. Even if the other person doesn't do the tasks perfectly, or in the exact same way you would do it, some of the tasks truly could be done by others.

One of the first tasks I wanted to get help with when I started my business was accounting and tax preparation. I'm just not an expert in this area, and I wanted to have an accountant who could take on these tasks right from the start. I've never regretted this decision. Over the years as my business has evolved, I've asked her and her team to take on other tasks such as some of the state forms that need to be filed and other required items.

She and her team send the prepared documents to me, with sticky notes that show me where I need to sign and a note about the check I may need to send with the forms. In their notes, they tell me when I need to mail it and they include an addressed envelope, so I can just sign, add the check, and mail it off. Having my accountant on my team gives me great support and saves me time that I would much rather devote to other business projects!

Types of Help and Support

Now that you've started your lists of business and household tasks that you might like to delegate, if possible, let's look at some of the options. Experiment to see which ones may suit you and your business and your family.

The first suggestion I want to offer may feel a bit radical, but it deserves a place on the list of options. Consider whether the tasks you would prefer not to do yourself can be done less often, done more quickly, or perhaps not even done at all. Use your good judgment with this question, of course! Toilets do need to be cleaned and dishes need to be washed and some types of papers need to be shredded and some papers need to be filed. Be willing to take a fresh look at your assumptions about who could do the tasks and how often they need to be done.

Next, think about who could help you with some of the tasks on your lists. It's easy to assume that the only choice would be to hire people to do these tasks. That certainly is one option, but there are several other possibilities.

There are some types of tasks that I do hire an expert to help with, like the CPA who helps with matters. I encourage you to have some of these professionals too. Think of it as forming your team that helps your life and your business succeed. For example, a web person can help with website work and a computer expert can help with your computers.

Beyond these types of professionals, think about the people who are already in your life. Who else in your household could help, even if it is only with parts of some of the tasks? Children can help with many simple tasks, starting at a young age and it is good for them to feel like they are part of the family and that they play an important role in the household. Other family members may be able to help with more involved tasks.

You may have neighbors you could exchange help with, particularly tasks they may be faster or better at than you. There may be tasks you could help them with, tasks that you don't mind doing, or you even enjoy doing. Perhaps you could share some home cooked meals with a neighbor and they could help with your yard work. Or, you and a neighbor could team up and split errands, with them returning your library books and you picking up their clothes at the cleaners.

Take a look at delivery services that are available in your community. In the past few months, I've been noticing that more and more stores in our area are starting to offer delivery services for free or for a small fee. Compare the fee or the tip you would give to the driver to the amount of time it would take for you to do the task. I'm excited to see the local grocery store where I prefer to shop has begun to offer delivery service. I plan to give it a try and I think it would save me time. On top of that, it would probably help me to avoid buying things that are not on my shopping list. I'll bet this alone could more than pay for the fee!

Remember to look for online options too, such as paying bills online, depositing checks through your mobile banking app, and ordering some of your supplies and materials. Some stores also offer the option to order online and pick things up quickly in the store. Go a step further and ask them what information is required for someone else besides you to be able to pick up the items. Usually they only need for you to indicate who will pick up the items and then that person will need to show identification when they pick up the order.

I do order some items online, especially things I can't find easily in local stores. I like to shop locally for some things to to support businesses in my area when possible. I aim for a balance between local purchases and online purchases. You'll want to think about what will work best for your situation.

Ask other entrepreneurs in your area about people and services they use. Be willing to try them when it makes sense and when they can help to streamline your tasks and help to boost your productivity.

Be the Leader of Your Team

You must be the leader of your business team. Often, we start our business as microbusinesses, or even as small side hustles in the extra hours we have during evenings or weekends after working at a traditional job. Over time, hopefully, the business grows. One of the important things that must also grow is seeing yourself as the leader of your business, the CEO of your enterprise. Yes, you may also fill other roles, but the first and most essential role is to be the head of your business.

It is very common for people to start a business doing a type of work that they are good at. They enjoy the work and want to be the main person doing it. You can design your business so that doing the work of the business is a large part of your business day. Be sure to include time and energy to focus on the leadership role too.

Being the CEO means having the mindset of a leader. This role includes things like thinking about goals for your business, planning for resources for your growing business, dealing with challenges that may arise, determining the policies and methods that guide your business. It is also up to you to select and give direction and lead people who provide services for your business. The more you do this, the more your business can be focused and productive.

Think about the outcomes you want to achieve from the work of each person who has a role in your business. Take time to discuss these outcomes with each person so they are clear about what you are expecting. Set and get agreement about due dates and interim checkpoints. You can ask for their ideas and advice about how to approach a task, but ultimately it is up to you to make the final decision about how you want things done for your business.

Set up regular times to touch base with each person about the progress they are making. This gives you opportunities to praise their progress and good work, or to give feedback to help make adjustments to be closer to the quality of work you are expecting. If you need to make a change, be professional and courteous in the way you communicate it. Be prompt about paying them for their services and keep good records and receipts.

Take some time each month and each quarter to set some new goals for your business. Some goals may be continuations of your current goals, while others may be new projects you want to pursue. Keep a list in your notebook about projects you would like to pursue, when the time is right. Keep a list of things to learn and books to read.

One thing I want to caution you about is the trap of continuing to add new projects without trimming some old projects. It's easy to end up feeling very busy and like you are going in too many directions at once.

One of my mentors has a great technique for this. He always starts the process of setting goals for the next year around the beginning of November. This enables him to get his goals solidified well before the end of year holidays. It also enables him to get things started very quickly at the beginning of each year. You may want to follow his model and start your goal setting earlier than the very end of the year.

He has another technique that he uses in this process that you may want to adopt too. He identifies approximately 15% of his current activities that he will complete or discontinue when the current year ends. This opens up 15% of the space in his time and in his mental energy to take on new projects and revenue streams that he is excited to launch. You may find this technique to be a great one to adopt for your business too!

As we wrap up this chapter, I hope you are already seeing some great possibilities for tasks that you can delegate to others or accomplish through team resources. And most important, I hope you are seeing how these adjustments can help to make room for more of the high value business tasks that are an excellent use of your time and energy as the leader of your business!

Section Four

How to Be Highly Productive Working At Home

Everything we have been talking about up to this point has been leading to this section of the book. In fact, you may have turned right to this section, looking for practical ideas and specific tips to increase your productivity as you work at home. You will find lots of great ideas here. I also want to encourage you to read the earlier chapters because each one has ideas and information that will help with many aspects of having an enjoyable and productive business at home.

In Section Four, I'll cover a wide variety of techniques from tiny adjustments to some big shifts that I hope you will find helpful as you continue to grow your business. Let each method or technique spark additional ideas. Implement some of them now and put other ideas on the back burner for consideration later.

In Chapter 9, I'll focus on your daily routines, and your daily action habits. These form the foundation for your business because they become the regular rhythm of activity that sets the tone and pace in your business.

In Chapter 10 I want to include some special methods that are particularly useful when you are tackling large or long-term projects. These kinds of projects will go more smoothly and successfully when you have strategies to handle them.

Chapter 11 addresses some of the family issues that affect almost every entrepreneur who works at home. These family factors change and evolve over time. They can have a big impact on your business, which may require you to make major adjustments to keep your business going.

We wrap up this section with Chapter 12 that covers the everyday challenges of distractions, procrastination, and times of low energy that can affect every entrepreneur. I'll provide ideas and techniques that can help you handle these issues and keep moving.

Chapter Nine

Daily Action and Productivity Strategies

Start with Your Goals

In Chapter 2, I encouraged you to set goals for your business. Ideally, you now have at least three short term 90-day goals, and three longer term 3-year goals. By having clarity about your business goals, you are in a good position to set up your days and weeks for high productivity. There are several ways to do this.

One of the simplest methods is to use a small tablet, about 5" by 7" in size. This is a good size to hold a short list and you are less likely to be tempted to write an unrealistically long list. Think about the top 3 to 5 business tasks that you need to accomplish today. Write these down on the small tablet and put it where you can see it as you work. You can make this the first thing you do each day as you start to work. Or, you may find it helpful to make this list at the end of the day for what you want to focus on the following day. This gets you ready to dive right in when you start working the next day. If you prefer to make an electronic list, I still recommend that you look at it regularly throughout your work day. Seeing the list gives you a visual reminder of your intentions for the day and it can help you get back on track when you need it.

You may be wondering why I suggest just 3 to 5 items for your daily list. It might not sound like very many tasks for the day. But I've been surprised how often it fits the reality of the day. Experiment for a few days to see if this is true for you as well. If you decide to make a little bit longer list, I still encourage you to identify the top five items so that you have a clear visual set of priorities for the day.

As you make your list, include action steps that are connected with your 90-day goals so that you make steady progress toward them each week. You may have other tasks that are on your list but build your core daily list around your 90-day goals. As you make progress on them, you will find that they naturally flow into your 3-year goals.

I encourage you to set some short and long-term goals for your personal life too. On a weekly basis, behind the scenes, keep a running list of personal tasks you want or need to accomplish. This helps to keep you moving toward your personal goals and it will also help to keep your household running smoothly.

Some of these personal tasks can fit into your break times during the day, especially things like 5 minutes of walking or watering your plants. It can also include things like phone calls that need to be made during business hours, such as calls to set or confirm appointments. I like to incorporate one or two of these personal tasks into my late afternoon timeframe when I am ready to take a longer break from work tasks.

Use the Power of Daily Rhythms and Routines

No matter how awesome your workspace is or how great your goals are for your business, ultimately you have to get the work done to achieve your goal of a successful business. One of the biggest secrets for success in your business is to develop a strong set of daily rhythms and routines that enable you to be productive getting things done.

Decide ahead of time when you will start your work day. This is one of the benefits of working at home. Some people like the routine of starting at the same time every day. This can begin to form a positive habit and connect the pattern in your brain. After just a few days, it will feel like it's time to start working and it may even feel strange if you don't. This can work to your advantage by creating a good work pattern that can serve you well.

Consider setting a timer for your first break too. Don't just work until you are exhausted. A principle that really works is to rest before you are tired. If you wait until you feel exhausted, it takes more time to feel refreshed and reenergized. A short break at a planned time can help to refresh your energy so that you can begin your next work task with a reserve of energy. Set a timer for the end of your break too, so that you can relax without having to keep an eye on the clock. If you use the timer or alarms on your mobile phone, choose a sound that is pleasing, and not startling, for your alarm sounds.

In an earlier chapter I described the option of working in a cycle of two 20-minute time chunks, followed by a 20-minute rest or enjoyment time chunk. The other cycle I see many entrepreneurs use is a 45 to 50-minute focused work chunk followed by a 10 to 15-minute rest break. These one-hour work/rest cycles can be repeated several times within each day, and you can tailor them to fit your work day. Whichever you choose, use it consistently to develop a rhythm for your work time.

Another great productivity strategy is to develop a morning routine. A well-planned morning routine can help to get your work day off to a good start. Two great resources that can provide ideas for your morning routine are Marla Cilley and Hal Elrod.

Marla Cilley (see her website at Flylady.net) focuses on having a simple morning routine that helps you get up and get going on a physical and household level. Her suggestions guide you to fine tune your morning routine to fit your life and your household. Her recommended morning routine includes things like getting dressed (including shoes), making the bed, giving your bathroom a quick tidying up, and starting a load of laundry.

Marla also suggests having an evening routine too. This can include having a wind down routine, giving your kitchen sink a quick cleanup and shine, and preparing a few things for a smooth morning the next day for you and your family.

Hal Elrod describes his morning routine in his book *The Miracle Morning.* It focuses on six key activities (SAVERS) including silence, affirmations, visualization, exercise, reading, and scribing (journaling). This morning routine can be shortened for busy days, or it can take longer if you have the time.

Notice when your peak energy time is during the day. If you are more of a morning person, use this knowledge to plan your mornings for high productivity on priority tasks. If your energy is higher in the afternoon or in the evening, plan your day to put more of your high priority tasks later in the day. Either way, the goal is to use your lower energy times for more routine tasks so that you can use your best mental energy times for your top priority work.

Even with the best designed schedules, there will be days when you'll need to shift to a "Plan B" schedule. This may occur because of a family issue, or a health situation, or an appointment that just can't be scheduled any other time.

For example, just this week, there are three appointments that I'll need to take a family member to. This isn't a task that I can delegate. I'll need to adjust my work routines to fit around these commitments. You probably have things like this that need to fit into your schedule, too. Preplanning and preparation are the answer to these kind of schedule issues.

In this case, I've mapped out the addresses for each appointment and estimated the time needed for driving. I will have some tasks that I can do on my mobile phone, because there will probably be some waiting time. I carry a small mobile charger with me in case I need to recharge my phone. I'll carry some protein snacks and a couple of bottles of water too.

While this isn't an ideal situation for getting a lot of work done on the days of the appointments, it still provides a way to make the best of the circumstances. I hope you will follow a similar process of planning and preparing in advance. Do the best you can, especially when there are predictable adjustments like these to your routines.

Another excellent productivity tool that fits in the category of rhythms and routines is to develop and use lists and checklists. They can help you be consistent in your approach, avoid forgetting things, and complete tasks faster because the checklist helps you to stay on track. Any task that you do often may benefit from creating a checklist. This can also be very helpful when you want to delegate tasks. The checklist lets the other person know the steps and actions you want to have completed.

An example of a list I use all the time is called a "Waiting For" list. This is a concept I first learned about in David Allen's classic book, *Getting Things Done*. The idea is simple and very useful. Anything that you are waiting for and which is not completed yet is a candidate for the list. This can include things like a call back, an assignment you asked someone else to work on, results from a test or an application, and many more. By writing the item on the Waiting For list, you can put it out of your immediate thoughts and focus on your priorities for the day. Check the list daily or weekly to track progress and to see if there are some items that need follow up.

Another type of list I use often is something I call the "After This" list. This is a list where I capture any task that I am not going to focus on right now and that I want to remember to do later. For example, whenever I travel, I use an "After This" list for things I want to remember to do after I return from the trip. Another time when I use an "After This" list is when I am working on a big project, such as writing this book. Ideas and other project possibilities are always popping into my mind. I use the "After This" list as a place to capture them so that I remember them and can consider them later after the deadline for my current project. This has really helped me to be less distracted by ideas and yet not forget them either.

Similarly, I like to keep a "Weekend List" of things I plan to do over the weekend. I jot down tasks as they occur to me so that I don't keep thinking about them. It also helps to keep me from getting distracted and doing those tasks during the week when it would be better if I was getting work tasks done.

Track Your Progress

As you develop your daily and weekly rhythms and routines, build in some ways to track your progress. One of the easiest and most powerful ways to do this is a quick end of the day routine. Take five minutes to write down what you accomplished during the day. I like to do this in my notebook, using a bullet style list format so that it is very quick to complete. I do this in two columns, one column for the business tasks I've worked on and one column for any personal tasks I've given time to. Over time, this daily review helps you to see your patterns of action and whether you are actually doing the things you were aiming to do. It can feel great to see all that you have accomplished!

Go a step further and take 15 minutes every week to look back over your daily results lists. Look for patterns. Were there certain days that were higher or lower in terms of your productivity? Did you find yourself gravitating to a particular project or goal? Or was there a goal or project that you seemed to avoid? Use these insights to adjust to your goals and plans for the week ahead.

At the end of each quarter (and each year) do a similar review but look especially at your progress on the 90-day goals you were working on. Which ones have you completed? Are some still unfinished? Notice and adjust as you set your next set of 90-day goals. Celebrate your progress and your successes!

Creating rhythms and routines as well as methods for tracking your progress are important parts of your daily Productivity Plan. They will support you in taking the effective and focused action that is one of the key secrets to achieving success. I encourage you to use and adapt these techniques and strategies to help you reach your goals!

Chapter Ten

Tackling Big or Extended Term Projects

Make a Plan

In chapter 9 we introduced many techniques for productive daily and weekly routines. In this chapter we're going to expand the focus to include productivity strategies for large scale and extended term projects.

For our purposes I'm going to define large projects as anything that is complex and has many parts. It may also take an extended amount of time to complete. Extended term projects are projects or tasks that occur over many weeks, months, or even years. It may be something repetitive that needs to be done on a regular basis, even though it may not be a very complex project. For example, keeping track of your business expenses is an extended term project that will continue for as long as you run your business.

In order to be productive with big or extended term projects start by developing a plan. Put your plan in writing, either in your notebook or on your computer. Start by identifying the key outcomes you want to achieve with this project. Then write down a series of goals that will be the big pieces needed to move toward these outcomes.

You may also find it helpful to break each of these goals into a series of smaller steps or sub goals that may fit into your short term 90-day goals. This will make it easier to plan the work schedule for the project.

Think about the sequence for the various chunks of your project. Some parts can be done simultaneously, and some will need to be completed before other parts can be started. With this information, you can begin to lay out a timeline for the various parts of the project.

Take your plans a step further and think about when you will actually fit the project work into your daily or weekly schedule. One of the secrets for success is to build in time to work on both your big and extended projects on a regular basis. If it helps you to have a big chunk of time to really focus on a project, you may want to devote a half day or even a full day at a time to a big project. Or if you prefer having more variety, you may want to put a focused hour on the big or extended project several times each week, allowing for other tasks and projects to fill the rest of your work time. Notice what works best for you. Don't keep working in a way that isn't giving you good productive results. Experiment and adjust until you find your best style and pattern to be truly productive with both your big projects and your daily tasks.

For example, it can be wise to schedule the time to work on a big project first thing on the days you are going to work on it, to give it some of your best focus and energy. Or if you are not a morning person, plan to use your best energy time during the day for the big project and do less intensive tasks during the other parts of the day.

As part of your plan, be sure to build in ways to celebrate your progress when you are working on big or extended projects. You can tie these celebrations to the sub goals within the project, or you can choose to celebrate whatever progress you have made each week or month.

Your celebrations don't have to be elaborate. Choose celebrations that are meaningful to you. Your celebration can be as simple as a special cup of tea, a special lunch or dinner, or purchasing an item that has been on your wish list. Or you can celebrate big accomplishments in a bigger way if you like.

Make it Visible

A key part of being productive with your big and extended projects is to track your progress toward the completion of the project. The goal is to mark your progress and to help you see how far you have come even though you may have many steps to go before the project is complete. Another important benefit of using a tracking system is to help strengthen your pattern of successful action over time in a way that you can readily see.

Choose tracking methods that fit your style and personality. For example, if you want a highly visible method, or if other people are involved, you may want to create a wall poster or a printed timeline and mark off steps completed. You can even use stars or stickers or big colorful sticky notes to show the progress. Or you can use a shared document online that each person can access.

You can also use a wall calendar or a small pocket calendar to make your progress visible. Use it to jot brief notes about daily progress made. You can also write a number that measures something related to your project in the square for each day. Or, you can just place a big checkmark on each day to show that you worked on the project that day. It can be very motivating to see a string of days with progress made!

You can combine several of these techniques. For example, as I am writing this book, which is definitely a big project, I keep a notebook where I write down the actions I take on it each day and the total number of words I write each day. Word documents make it easy to see how many words I am writing. Because I have chosen a tight timeline for writing the book, my goal is to write 1000 words most days.

Another simple yet very powerful method for tracking progress and making it visible is to use something I call a

"Success Indicator." I like to use old fashioned lined index cards (white or colors) for this, but you could create and print out a simple chart in Word or Excel too.

On the left-hand side of the card, I write down actions or habits that I want to focus on and track. Then I draw vertical lines across the rest of the card, so I have a small column for each day of the week. The actions and habits on your card can be a mix of personal and business-related items. For example, you could list exercising, using dental floss, posting business things on social media, or writing a regular blog post.

This little index card is easy to carry in a pocket or to tuck into a folio or to place on your desk. Keeping it visible will remind you to focus on the tasks or habits you have chosen as you go through each day. You can place checkmarks or tick marks or stars to track how often or how much you are doing of the items on your Success Indicator. It gives you a quick, easy visual indicator of your actions and your progress. It will also help you to see gaps or strings of successful days.

You can create a fresh Success Indicator each week. Many of the items from one week may be things you will want to focus on during the next week too. This is such a simple method, but it is very powerful. You may want to experiment to see how it could help you to boost your focus and your productivity.

Get Support and Resources

Another great secret for success with big projects is to enlist an accountability partner. Set up a regular time when you will communicate with them to let them know about your progress. Just knowing that you will be telling someone else about your progress can be very powerful in helping you to stay in productive action. It feels good to tell them that you have made progress and not so good to tell them that you are off track. Use this extra bit of connection and support to help you stay in motion.

A very simple arrangement can be to have an agreement that you will send a text message or an email to your accountability partner at agreed upon time intervals. This can be daily or weekly. Agree ahead of time what kind of response you would like from your accountability partner and find out if this is something they are able and willing to do. Make it something that will be easy for both of you to do or it will be hard to sustain it.

Another great option to support your success with big projects is to engage the support of a coach. A good coach can help you as you develop plans, create action strategies, define accountability methods, and even guide you with troubleshooting and making adjustments over time as your big projects unfold. This type of support can help you to make steady progress on your big projects. I really enjoy working with clients who have big projects they are working on. It's exciting to see them make rapid progress!

Joining a mastermind group is another excellent option for having great support for your big projects. A mastermind is a small group of people who meet on a regular basis, either in person or by phone or videoconference. Each person in the group is committed to supporting and encouraging the other members as they move forward with their most important projects. I have been a part of several mastermind groups. In fact, I have organized several mastermind groups over the years too, because they are so helpful in making progress on big projects.

It is very powerful to tap into the wisdom and experience of the people in your mastermind. Seeing each person's progress and celebrating their successes is motivating for everyone in the group. It offers the excellent benefit of the diverse experience of each person in the group. Just knowing that you will meet with the group on a regular basis can give you an extra boost of energy to help you stay in action and to achieve high levels of productivity.

As you can see, having productive strategies for working on your big projects or your extended term projects can make a big difference in completing them successfully. I encourage you to design some big projects as part of working toward your most important business goals. Use the techniques in this chapter to help you accomplish them. Review your progress regularly and celebrate your wins along the way!

Chapter Eleven

Family Factors Matter, Especially When You Work at Home

Set Up Family Rhythms and Routines

Many people work from home to have the flexibility to help or care for other family members. This can include children, grandchildren, partners and spouses, parents, or even grandparents. Working at home when other family members are involved requires some special strategies.

The first thing to do is to look at your schedule to establish times for work and times for family. Think about the amount of time you need to schedule for work tasks, and the amount of time you need for family care or support. It will probably require some determination and focus to be sure you have time for both.

If you are a morning person, you may want to get up before the rest of the family so that you have time to focus on work tasks before the rest of the household is up. By contrast, if you are more of a night owl, it may work well for you to schedule some of your work time at night after your household is quiet. You may also need time in the middle of the day when you can schedule client appointments, meetings, or networking events.

Plan and schedule regular time to focus on your work. The schedule you lay out will have to flex and adjust at times to meet family and caregiving needs. But if you have a core schedule in place it gradually becomes the normal expected routine, both for yourself and for your family.

A strategy that works well for some people is to have one or two days when you work an extended schedule. This could be one larger block of time or two three-hour blocks with a break in the middle of the day. You may even choose to work away from your home on these days, going to a place like the library, a co-working space, or a coffee shop to reduce the possible distractions of home. If your budget permits, you may want to arrange for extra family support on a day like this, so that you can focus your time on your work with less risk of family interruptions or distractions.

Be willing to experiment with various schedules and options until you find a solution that works reasonably well for you and your family. Set your schedule and then work with it for three or four weeks, or even longer, to give it a good trial. Then evaluate what worked and what didn't so that you can fine tune it.

Establish Boundaries and a Plan B

Whatever core schedule you put in place, you'll need to be ready to flex to a 'Plan B' schedule when business or family needs don't go as planned. Realize that some of this is normal because people are involved, and things come up. Your family's needs can vary and can even be somewhat unpredictable. Someone may get a cold or have some other health challenge. You may have three client projects that all come through at the same time. So, it's smart to have a backup plan as well. Think about how you can accommodate these different needs.

Learn how to tell when you truly need to adjust and flex your schedule and when you need to keep a boundary with your family members. Setting and keeping good boundaries is an essential part of being productive when you work at home. As important as boundaries are, it can be a challenge to set them and to keep them.

The purpose of boundaries, in this situation, is to protect your time and space and quiet for getting your work done. You may need to set boundaries about your workspace and who can enter during your work hours, or who can put things in your work area.

A smart boundary to put in place is to establish specific "quiet times" or "focus times." These are chunks of time when you ask other people to respect your need for work time and to plan their times to talk with you either before or after your designated work times.

With family members, it is wise to set very clear starting and ending times for your work so that they know when you are available and when you are not to be disturbed. Define what constitutes a valid "emergency" that warrants an interruption during your focus time. If you don't do this, you risk receiving many interruptions and you'll probably end up feeling frustrated and unproductive. With boundaries, your intention needs to be very clear: your work time is important, and it needs to be valued and respected.

Think about creative solutions that can help your family members to respect your boundaries. For example, you could set up a bulletin board or a dry erase white board on your door or in the family living area where people can write messages or a reminder about things they want to discuss with you. This gives them a way to capture their thoughts while they are fresh in their minds but without needing to interrupt you in the process. Follow through by looking at the board for messages and responding as soon as your focus time is finished.

Another good strategy that helps with boundaries is to have a separate area or room where you work, if possible. If you are trying to work at the kitchen table while other family members are around, it will be almost impossible to prevent interruptions. So, choose your work location with some thought about a place that will support your efforts to be focused and productive.

Hang a cute or funny sign on the door to help remind the people around you that this is work time and that you are not to be disturbed. Put a sticky note on it that has the time when you'll be available for conversation.

Another good strategy is to think about ways to minimize interruptions. Use the restroom before you start working. You may want to keep some water and some almonds or a protein bar in your work area so that you don't need to get up during your focus time.

As your work and family situation changes over time, your boundaries will need to be reviewed and possibly adjusted too. Look for ways to enlist your family members to support your efforts. Talk about the ways your work makes a positive impact on your family.

It is up to you to set the boundaries and to communicate them. In some situations, this can be done collaboratively, reaching an arrangement that is good for everyone. In some situations, such as with children or with a resistant older person, it will be up to you to establish the boundaries and to be assertive in enforcing them.

Plan for Relaxation, Fun, and Family Time

Ultimately, when family members are a part of your work at home picture, the secret to success involves developing a sense of rhythm and balance. Every day may be a bit different, depending on what's happening in the family. Your Productivity Plan needs to allow for this. Most families thrive when there are rhythms and routines as a foundation of the schedule. This includes planning for your work time and space, but also developing rhythms and routines for your non-work time as well.

Preplan some activities that would be enjoyable to do with your family. This could be a play break or a storybook with a child, a phone call with an older family member to check on their wellbeing and to ask about their day. It could also be ending your work day at a preplanned time that family members know to expect, and then preparing for supper together, or time in the evening to relax and unwind together.

Involve your family members in planning for fun and enjoyable activities. Use a family calendar to mark dates for activities. A big part of the pleasure for everyone is in anticipating the fun. The more they can see that there are regular, planned times when you'll be engaged with them, away from your work, the more like they are likely to be supportive of your work efforts.

Chapter Twelve

Successful Ways to Handle Common Challenges

Tackle the Distractions

Distractions are some of the most common challenges that every entrepreneur faces when they choose to work at home. Working in a traditional office can have distractions too, but when you work at home it's completely up to you to address them and find solutions for them. In this chapter, I'll share several successful strategies.

The first kinds of distractions that you may face, often on a daily or even hourly basis, are the many household distractions that are all around you in your home. You probably have a list of things that need to be done around the house and thinking about these tasks can tug at your focus.

This can be intensified if the tasks at home feel urgent or very important in some way. A simple example of this is a telephone ringing that you may feel you should answer, rather than letting it go to the voicemail system. Or the doorbell rings and you are curious about who is there or if a package is being delivered.

Use your notebook and take inventory of the kinds of distractions that you experience most often. It could be household tasks like the dishes or the laundry, or it could be seeing a stack of work papers that need to be sorted and filed. It could be wanting to get up and get a snack or cup of tea or coffee. It could even be seeing a spot on the floor or on the window that suddenly bothers you and just "needs" to be cleaned even though it wasn't bothering you the evening before. That's just how distractions work!

Other distractions can be a bit more subtle. There are always tasks that need to be done in any business. This is just part of being an entrepreneur. It is very easy to be distracted by simpler or less important work tasks when there are higher priority tasks that need your attention. It can be easy to get pulled into looking at email or checking social media. While these tasks can be useful for your business, it's easy to spend more time on them than you may have intended to.

Another curious thing that you have probably noticed is the way distractions can feel more intense if the business task you need to be doing is unpleasant or uncomfortable or unfamiliar. It is easy to be distracted by something else that seems like it would be easier or more important or more enjoyable or as an escape from the priority task at hand. Have you ever found yourself playing just one more round of your favorite game when there is a big business task that you really need to be working on?

Here are some of my favorite strategies for handling distractions. See which ones work best for you.

When you work at home, you have your business materials and equipment around you as well as all of your household furniture and possessions. There are lots of potential visual distractions. If you find that seeing things at home is part of the distraction factor for you, then you may find that you can boost your productivity by working in a part of your house that has fewer visual distractions. This could be a separate room where you can close the door.

You may also want to experiment with changing the direction your desk or table faces, so that you have fewer things in your field of vision. For example, I have a work table set up so that I am looking out a window at a quiet part of my yard. There is almost nothing else in my line of sight when I sit at that table. This gives me a view of the sky and a tree and some shrubs which is peaceful, and it eliminates the visual distractions of the other parts of the house.

When I am feeling susceptible to distractions and I have a high priority task to work on, I often leave the house to work somewhere else for a few hours. My favorite places include a coffee shop or a cafe near my house. I prefer to choose places that take less than 10 minutes to get to, so that I have more work time and less travel time to get there.

Some people like the library, especially if they can use a desk or table tucked away in a quiet corner. If you are in a large city you may have several branch libraries or even college libraries where you could work. Another option is to find a co-working space where you can pay a day rate to be able to work at one of their tables or rooms. Choose a place that has a level of noise or quiet that works best for you. Experiment with several locations so that you have options when you need them.

If you must stay at home and work, there are several strategies you may find helpful to reduce the lure of distractions. Use the timer techniques in this book to help you focus in on your work tasks. Promise yourself that you will give yourself a short break afterward to do something you would otherwise consider a distraction. Set a timer for that too, and when it sounds, switch back to your work task. This is a variation of the timer techniques we talked about earlier in the book. The idea is, instead of fighting the distraction, you work with it and build it into your work routine. This takes some of the energy out of the distraction and you may find it helps you to feel the satisfaction of getting both your work task underway and the "distraction" task too.

Another great technique is to enlist an accountability partner and use the "bookend technique." This person can be a friend or a colleague who is willing to be in this role for you that day. Set up the idea of this arrangement with them ahead of time so that you both agree about how it will work. You may also want to return the favor for them later, when they need similar support.

Here is the process: Call or text the person and tell them in a brief sentence or phrase the name of the work task you will be focusing on for the next chunk of time. Don't go into much detail as that can be a distraction too! You can say simply "I'm going to work on a business task for the next 45 minutes" without even naming the task. At the end of your work time, send them a quick message to let them know that you worked on it for 45 minutes, again without going into any details. You are just doing a brief check in to complete the cycle.

The "bookend" idea comes from the fact that you are briefly connecting with them right before and right after you work on the task, like bookends on either side of a set of books on a shelf. This simple but powerful technique can be just the extra leverage you need to help yourself get focused and stay focused on the business task that needs to be done. It helps to know that someone else knows that you intend to be working and that you will be connecting with them afterward.

By knowing what some of your most common distractions are, you can plan strategies to help you manage them. Some distractions can be reduced or eliminated, but there will always be some distractions that you have to deal with. By having awareness of the ones that you are most prone to, and having strategies that you can turn to, you can still be effective and productive in getting work done at home.

Overcome Procrastination

Procrastination is an issue that almost all of us face at one time or another. Procrastination is, by definition, putting off doing a task which ideally should be done now.

There are lots of reasons why people procrastinate. You may procrastinate because you don't really want to do the higher priority task. Perhaps you aren't exactly sure how to do the task that you are putting off. You may worry that the task you are delaying will be unpleasant in some way. Or perhaps you are feeling pressured by someone to do a task or by some external requirement and you resist by procrastinating.

Awareness of your own patterns with procrastination is a great starting point for developing effective strategies for preventing or overcoming it. Take a few minutes to think about the kinds of tasks that you sometimes procrastinate doing. This is another good time to grab your notebook and capture these thoughts. For example, writing is not my favorite thing to do. I would much rather talk than have to take the time to sit and compose words on the computer. It is a task that I often procrastinate doing, even though there are many benefits to writing. Another thing that I sometimes procrastinate doing is routine tasks like filing and organizing papers and doing bookkeeping.

A more subtle layer of awareness is to identify the kinds of activities you do when you are procrastinating. The various types of distractions that I mentioned at the beginning of this chapter can sometimes be the things we do when we are procrastinating about doing something else that is a higher priority now. For myself, I do things like getting a snack, doing a different work task that isn't the one I really need to be doing, and even doing routine housework tasks like folding the laundry or sweeping the floor. Sometimes I'll check my email, call a friend, or sit and watch some television. None of these things are bad things in and of themselves. But I have observed myself doing them enough times that I can tell when I am actually just procrastinating about doing something more important. Have you observed this kind of procrastination behavior in yourself too?

The more you can notice the patterns in your life and business, the better you will be able to find strategies for addressing your particular situation. Sometimes just noticing and admitting to yourself that you are procrastinating is enough to help you shift into productive action. But it's not always that easy to break out of the pattern. I want to share some additional strategies that may be helpful. (If you want even more ideas and techniques, I also recommend that you look at my earlier book, *No More Procrastination! Get Into Action, Achieve Your Goals!*)

First, ask yourself if this is a task that someone else could help you with, or whether someone else could even do the whole thing for you. If this is an option, consider the possibility of delegating it. In my own business, I have gotten help with organizing papers as well as help with bookkeeping tasks. What a relief to not have to do all of it myself!

For the tasks that you decide you still must do, use the technique I've described of writing down the top 3 to 5 things that are most important for you to work on today. Writing them out is an important part of this strategy. When you can see them written out on a tablet or in your notebook, it helps you to be clearer about which tasks you've chosen as your top priorities for the day.

Start with the one task on this list that is the most important one and begin your work day by focusing on that task before you do any other work. Give it at least 30 to 60 minutes of focused effort before you stop and take a break. Then get up and move around for five to fifteen minutes. Come back and do another 30 to 60 minutes of focused work on that same task or on the second task on your top priority list. Often, seeing the progress you can make in just one or two cycles of focused effort is enough to help you get past the desire to procrastinate.

Another great technique is to focus on how good it will feel to have an hour of work completed on your top task. For example, you may feel a sense of accomplishment, or just a sense of relief. Either way, imagine the feeling vividly. Let it help to pull you forward to do the task so that you can enjoy the reward of the feeling.

If imagining the good feeling of progress or completion doesn't energize you to do the task, then you can use a different type of reward. Do this by pairing up two tasks, one that you are procrastinating doing and one that you enjoy doing. Focus on the priority task first for 30 to 60 minutes. Then let yourself switch to the more enjoyable task for 30 to 60 minutes. You can cycle back and forth between tasks you may be procrastinating and more enjoyable tasks. Remember that the enjoyable task can be a work task. Or you can choose a personal task or activity that is relaxing and enjoyable. By switching back and forth, you make progress on the procrastinated task, but you do it in manageable chunks of time. Plus, you know that it will be followed by something more enjoyable.

A related technique is to add a layer of enjoyment or pleasure to the task that you are procrastinating. For example, listen to music that you enjoy while you work on a task you have been avoiding. If the task requires focus and concentration, it is best to choose music without lyrics. You can even add multiple layers of enjoyment. In addition to music you could have a fan blowing cool air on you, if that is something you enjoy. You could sip a cup of your favorite tea or wear a favorite sweater or keep a lovely flower in a vase on your desk. By adding a layer or two of extra pleasure you connect the less pleasurable task with things you know you enjoy. This can make it easier to do the task you are avoiding. As a result, you may find that you start to look forward to the task because you get the pleasure with it too.

A fascinating thing sometimes starts to happen as you make progress on a task you have been procrastinating about doing, It sometimes loses its procrastination pull. You may even begin to feel excited that you are making headway toward completing the task. At some point you can feel the momentum start to build as you are well into the task. And as you approach and pass the midpoint of the task, you can start to see that you are well on your way to completing it. This is cause for celebration! Enjoy this if it happens! But even if it doesn't, celebrate the fact that you are making steady progress and that you are doing the task even if it isn't your favorite.

Address Low Energy

The third type of challenge that can happen when you work at home is encountering times when your energy is low. If this is because you are feeling slowed by distractions or because you are procrastinating about doing something, use the strategies we've discussed already in this chapter. But you may also experience times of low energy because of health reasons or isolation or even overworking.

If health reasons are part of your low energy, please be sure to consult with your healthcare team to see if there are things that can be treated with their help and guidance. Your healthcare providers are part of your success team. Ask them what you can do to keep your health as vibrant as possible.

Be sure that you are following good self-care routines like the ones we covered in chapter 7 about staying healthy and energized when you work at home. It can be easy to fall into habits or patterns of overwork or long hours, especially when you are an entrepreneur. Let yourself take time away from work on a regular basis. This doesn't have to be a fancy vacation. It can be as simple as taking a half or a full day off each week to relax and refresh yourself.

Feeling isolated when you work at home can show up as low energy too. If possible, plan ahead for at least two or three opportunities to get out of the house each week. This can be for business related activities like attending workshops or going to networking events or participating in professional associations. You may also have opportunities to call on current or prospective clients who are in your area.

One of my colleagues enjoys volunteering. Her approach is to volunteer for a couple of hours in the afternoon one or two days a week. She completes several hours of work at home each morning. She can feel good knowing that she has accomplished quite a bit each day before she leaves the house. Volunteering helps her to feel energized and it connects her with other people in her community.

Another friend, Jean, lives out in the country. It takes about an hour for her to drive in to town. She plans one day each week when she will go into town and do several things. She often schedules a mix of activities like business networking events, personal appointments, and meetings with clients or colleagues. This gives her some time out of the house that she can look forward to each week and she does it in a planned and organized way to make the most of her time.

Finally, look for creative ways to have fun and laughter in your life to boost your energy. This can involve simple things like pursuing a hobby you enjoy, playing with your dog or cat, or watching funny movies. Schedule a date night or a fun activity with your family. Plan a time to get together with a friend or a neighbor for a walk or for a cup of coffee. Plan ahead for the weekend so that you have enjoyable things to look forward to rather than just letting the time slip away.

The more you can stay energized, and reduce distractions and procrastination, the more productive you are likely to be each day!

SECTION FIVE

WHAT'S NEXT ON YOUR WORK AT HOME JOURNEY?

In this final section, we'll talk about where to go from here. I hope you have already found some great ideas and strategies, ideas that have helped to boost your productivity in many ways. In this section we'll talk about ways to keep growing your business as your life and your business evolve. This is a key set of skills for long term business success.

When I work with clients I always like to ask them to think forward five to ten years and to imagine the changes that are likely to occur as they become five or ten years older. We also think about their children and other family members advancing in age five to ten years. By thinking about these changes that we can realistically anticipate, we can shape goals with these things in mind.

Whatever the future brings, I encourage you to be optimistic and to look for workable options. This will help you to grow through the changes and to adjust to the new circumstances so that you can continue to be productive and successful.

Chapter Thirteen

The Next Stage: When Things Change or Evolve

Your Productivity Plan Will Evolve Over Time

I have good news and bad news for you. The bad news is that the productivity strategies that are working well for you now will need to change and evolve over time. Even the ones that work the very best may need to be adjusted as your business and your situation at home change. I want to reassure you, though, that this is a normal part of business and life. The good news is that taking a fresh look and making some changes in your approach to your work can actually have very positive results for you.

I encourage you to be proactive. Do a regular review of your scheduling, your work locations, your portability options, and your use of technology. The end of each year and the midyear point at the end of June are natural times to review and refresh your business goals as well as your work methods and strategies.

The other times that are smart choices for this type of review is whenever changes occur in your business or in your personal life. These changes can include health changes, family changes, changes in the mix of revenue streams in your business, moving to a new home, as well as decisions to scale up to full time work or back to part time work.

One of my coaching clients, Ann, recently moved to a different part of the country when her husband made a major career change. This meant that she needed to meet people and find clients in her new location so that her business could continue to grow and thrive. We coached about ways to find local networking groups and events that would be a good match for the types of services she provides.

Then we looked at ways to adjust her daily and weekly work plan to fit these kinds of activities as well as the follow-up actions into her schedule. We took into account the quiet times when she would be the only person at home during the day, and the weekends when her husband would be at home. She lives near her grandchildren now, so she wanted to be able to have them visit regularly, staying at her home.

Ann was able to set up a bedroom with a corner that is devoted to work space for her business. She also decided to find a co-working style work space away from home that she can use occasionally by paying a daily rate. This helps her to maintain her productivity when her children and grandchildren are visiting and staying at her home. She is also able to use the co-working space to meet with clients when needed, rather than have them come to her house. By making these adjustments, Ann has been able to get her business up and running in her new city. She can accommodate visits with her family and still have access to a quiet work space during their extended visits.

Another client, Rhonda, recently let go of the leased office space she had been using for her business. She had been working from home occasionally, but this change meant she is now fully home-based with her business. This change saved her a fair amount of money on rent and utilities, as well as travel time going to her office. She already had a work area set up at home, so she is able to continue to use this space for her business activities. She is a naturally outgoing person, so part of our coaching has been around adjusting her schedule to include more activities away from her home and with other people. She is scaling back her work hours to a part time schedule as she is approaching retirement. This gives her time to go to exercise classes, meet friends for lunch, and take trips to visit her daughter. These actions have added to her joy in life while allowing her to continue to be productive with her part time business at home.

In the years ahead, take time regularly for take a fresh look at how you are using your work time and the way you have set up your work space. Talk with other entrepreneur friends and colleagues to ask how they handle situations similar to yours. Often, they will have ideas or can share examples that may work for you as well.

Stay Current with Trends, Resources, and Technology

Regularly review the equipment and technology you use. Watch the new trends, read about them, and then decide if it is something that is worth adopting. This allows time for bugs to be worked out and for support resources to be developed too. It also lets you plan when to put the investment into your business budget.

At the same time, I encourage you not to be the last person to adopt new technology either. There are many ways that new tools and resources can help you to be even more productive in your business.

Every time you purchase a new piece of business equipment or download a new app to use, it brings both opportunities and challenges. The opportunity is the possibility of streamlining your work. The challenge is that each one will take time to learn and to put it into regular use. Allow for this extra time in your schedule and be patient with yourself as you go through this initial learning phase.

If you need help don't be afraid to ask for it. You may have friend or a colleague who can make the process faster or easier.

People are often glad to share their knowledge if you ask, and I encourage you to return the favor to them or to someone else along the way.

Another great resource that can be quick and easy when you are learning or when you have a question is to do a quick search on Google or on YouTube for help or information. You can often find a blog post or a video that can answer your questions or provide a demonstration that will accelerate your learning process.

Find your best way to approach the process of adding new equipment and technology as you grow your business. Allow the extra time it takes to reach a comfort level with new things. Focus on the benefits you believe it can provide for you rather than on the time or frustration of having to learn new things. This will help you to keep moving forward, growing and evolving and staying current, which is part of the secret of business success.

Always Design It to Fit You!

Ultimately, it's up to you to choose the best tools and equipment for your business, the best options for setting up your work space, and the best strategies to productively run your business. I encourage you to always design it to fit yourself and your family.

Use your notebook as a place to capture ideas that you may want to consider, either now or in the future. Evaluate them in light of your current circumstances to see which will best serve you. It is completely okay and even necessary to make changes in your business as your circumstances change.

Recently, my colleague Jenny has begun to make changes in her business because of changes in her family situation. She is developing online information products, books, courses and webinars that will better fit her changing schedule. She is excited because these are also ways that she can reach and help more people. It's taking extra time and energy to learn how to do this but she is finding that she is enjoying the process. She is already starting to see some good results in her business. This is encouraging her to keep going with this evolution to her business.

My hope is that you will look at your business in a similar way. Think about the options that will let you take care of your family responsibilities while also achieving your business goals. You may have "seasons" where you need to focus more on your family and other times when you can focus more intensely on your business.

A business woman I know literally shifts her business into a slower "summer" mode when her young children are out of school during the summer. She is very open with her clients and customers that this is her priority. She plans her projects and programs to fit around this schedule. During the fall and spring when her kids are in school, she places more focus on her business. You can also do something similar around holidays that are important to your family such as the time between late November and the first of the year. It will require some planning and communication but it can be done!

Let yourself think and dream about the possibilities that you can create when you design your business to truly suit your needs and your style. Enjoy the ongoing evolution of your business. Celebrate your wins and enjoy each step forward! I look forward to hearing about your successes!

Conclusion

Congratulations for reading this book! I hope you have found encouragement as well as specific techniques and strategies that will help you be highly productive with your business at home.

Be open to continually improving your work methods as well as finding ways to increase your satisfaction and enjoyment with working at home. When changes occur in your family or your health or your business, don't get stuck feeling frustrated about them. It is normal for these kinds of changes to happen, and every entrepreneur experiences a variety of challenges over their years in business.

The secret is in how you approach these changes. The more you can remain positive and optimistic, the more likely it is that you will be able to find ways to adapt your business and your life to work with the changes.

In fact, I encourage you to look for ways you can make things even better, in unexpected ways, because of the need to make changes. A shift in your circumstances can often be the perfect catalyst to make some excellent changes in your business.

I hope that the ideas in this book will be a helpful resource as you work to achieve your exciting business goals. Aim high and enjoy making your work-at-home experience a great part of your life!

About the Author

Leslie Cardinal is a coach, mentor, speaker, and workshop facilitator as well as a published author. For more than 25 years, she has worked with leaders and entrepreneurs in a wide variety of industries guiding them to make rapid progress toward their professional goals.

Leslie draws on her unique background in industrial engineering, leadership development, coaching, and career success strategies to give her clients a unique advantage when they work with her to accelerate their successes.

This is her third book about strategies to achieve professional success. Her earlier books include ***I Hate to Be Late! Great Strategies to Help You Be On Time***, and ***No More Procrastination: Get Into Action, Achieve Your Goals!***

Learn more by visiting **LeslieCardinal.com**.
You can claim your free resources at
TheAtHomeProductivityBook.com